AMERICAN BEAUTY

Alan Ball (screenwriter/co-producer) counts *American Beauty* as his first produced feature film screenplay. He has already enjoyed great success in the television arena, and is creator, head writer, and executive producer of the comedy series *Oh Grow Up*.

Previously, Ball wrote for the hit series *Cybill* for three seasons, eventually becoming co-executive producer. He first made his name in television when he was offered a job writing for *Grace Under Fire* after producing partners Tom Werner and Marcy Carsey read one of his plays.

Prior to moving to Hollywood to work on *Grace Under Fire*, Ball was a playwright in New York. Among his credits are *Five Women Wearing the Same Dress*, which premiered in 1993 at Manhattan Class Company and starred

Thomas Gibson, Ally Walker, and Allison Janney; *The M Word*, which premiered at the inaugural Lucille Ball Festival of New American Comedy in 1991; *Made For a Woman*; *Bachelor Holiday*; *The Amazing Adventures of Tense Guy*; *Your Mother's Butt*; *Power Lunch*; and *The Two Mrs. Trumps*. He was also a founding member of Alarm Dog Rep, where he wrote, acted in, and directed a variety of revues and plays.

Born in Atlanta, Ball was raised in Marietta, Georgia. He attended Florida State University, where he majored in theatre with an emphasis in acting and playwriting. After college he moved to New York City, where he worked as an art director at *Adweek* and *Inside PR* magazines.

Sam Mendes (director), one of today's most celebrated theatre directors, has mounted award-winning productions on the stages of London, New York, and around the world. *American Beauty* marks his feature film directorial debut.

Mendes's many triumphs include the acclaimed revival of the musical *Cabaret*, first in London and then on Broadway. The latter production garnered four Tony Awards, including one for Best Revival of a Musical, three Drama Desk Awards, and three Outer Critics Circle Awards. He also directed *The Blue Room* on Broadway, starring Nicole Kidman. Mendes had previously directed the award-winning London production of *The Rise and Fall of Little Voice*, introducing Jane Horrocks, who reprised her role in the film version, *Little Voice*.

Born in England, Mendes was educated at Cambridge University and joined the Chichester Festival Theatre following his graduation in 1987. Soon after, he directed Dame Judi Dench in *The Cherry Orchard*, for which he won a Critics Circle Award for Best Newcomer. He then joined the Royal Shakespeare Company in 1990, where he directed such productions as *Troilus and Cressida* with Ralph Fiennes, *Richard III*, and *The Tempest*, for which he earned an Olivier Award nomination.

In 1992, Mendes became artistic director of the reopened Donmar Warehouse in London. There he has directed numerous award-winning productions, including the aforementioned *Cabaret*, and *The Glass Menagerie* and *Company*, for each of which he won the Olivier Award for Best Director. His other work at the Donmar includes *Assassins*, which won a Critics Circle Award, *Translations*, *Glengarry Glen Ross*, *Habeas Corpus*, and *The Front Page*.

His credits elsewhere include *The Sea* and *The Plough and the Stars*, both with Judi Dench; *The Birthday Party*; and *Othello*, which toured the world and for which he received another Olivier Award for Best Director.

Alan Ball

AMERICAN BEAUTY

FOUR

First published 1999 by Newmarket Press, New York.

This edition published 2000 by FilmFour Books
an imprint of Macmillan Publishers Ltd,
25 Eccleston Place, London SW1W 9NF
Basingstoke and Oxford

www.macmillan.co.uk

Associated companies throughout the world

ISBN 0 7522 7192 X

9 8 7 6

A CIP catalogue record for this book is available from the British Library.

Typeset by Blackjacks
Printed and bound in Great Britain by Mackays of Chatham plc, Chatham, Kent

ACKNOWLEDGMENTS
The publisher wishes to thank the following people who made an invaluable
contribution to this book: Alan Ball, Susan Bennett, Sharon Black, Joyce Brouwers,
Andrew Cannava, Bruce Cohen and Dan Jinks, Tara B. Cook, Kristy Cox, Anne
Globe, Margo Lane, Sam Mendes, Esperanza Perez, Boyd Peterson, Terry Press,
Dorit Saines, Michael Vollman and Stephanie Wheeler.

DreamWorks extends a special thanks to Esther Margolis, John Cook, Tom Perry,
and the rest of the staff at Newmarket Press who believed in the project and
worked at breakneck speed to make this book possible.

Introduction
by Sam Mendes

I first read *American Beauty* sitting on a plane travelling between Los Angeles and New York. I finished it and read it again. I arrived in New York, called my agent, Beth, and told her that I wanted to make the movie. Then I read it again. Normally it was a trial for me to get through a script once, and I'd read this one three times back to back. I wanted to know why this was. So I read it again.

The strange thing was that at each reading the script seemed to be something else. It was a highly inventive black comedy. It was a mystery story with a genuine final twist. It was a kaleidoscopic journey through American suburbia, and a hugely visually articulate one at that. It was a series of love stories. It was about imprisonment in the cages we all make for ourselves and our hoped-for escape. It was about loneliness. It was about beauty. It was funny. It was angry, very angry sometimes. It was sad. One thing I was certain of, the script, like its characters, wasn't at all what it first appeared.

Our relationship with the characters shifted and changed. What was this man Lester doing? Acting like a spoiled child or raging against the dying of the light? His wife Carolyn? Furious and frigid, yet vulnerable and lost. Jane? Impassive, unreadable, but with a well of tenderness barely visible to the naked eye. And Ricky. His camera emotionlessly recording its subject or reaching out to touch it? In the end my feelings about the finished movie and the script are indivisible. I love it (I'm biased, of course), but I still don't know how it *works*. With me, and also I suspect with Alan, instinct was my strongest and only guide.

One thing I did know on those initial readings, however, was that the writer wasn't scared to leave the characters alone with themselves; he seemed to know them well enough to allow them that privilege. Indeed, many of my favourite passages from the finished movie involve these moments of solitariness, caught by the camera's impassive and uninflected gaze. Carolyn in the empty sale house, putting herself back together again; Jane studying her reflection in the mirror after her mother has hit her; Ricky similarly alone in his room cleaning the blood from his face; Angela sitting on the stairs crying, with the rain outside; and of course Lester gazing at the image of his family, seeing it all clearly as it were, at the moment before his own death. Indeed, the voice that hovers over the movie seems to be the ultimate spiritual extension of that: Lester at once alone and at peace with himself, yet missing, genuinely missing, his 'little life'.

The movie was, of course, to repeat the old adage, extensively reshaped in the cutting room. A framework involving Ricky and Jane being tried and convicted of Lester's murder seemed clever but a mite cynical and at odds with Lester's spirit taking wing. This was excised along with any indications of the Colonel's ambivalent sexual feelings and other signposts that softened the movie's unexpected plot twists and changes of tone. Other changes were not so considered. The scene with Ricky and Jane walking home down the avenue of trees, for example, was written at the last minute to save us money and time, and turned out better than the scene it replaced. But it would be wrong to suggest that the film was ever in need of major surgery: Alan wrote it from the heart as well as the head, and it made it on to the screen with remarkably little interference from outside forces, other than the constant and unstinting support of producers Dan Jinks and Bruce Cohen, its torch bearers from the very beginning.

Of course, a whole set of additional presences enriched the movie. The extraordinary artistry and humanity of cinematographer Conrad Hall, the beautiful music of Tom Newman, along with the work of countless others, not to mention the huge contributions made by Kevin, Annette, Chris, Allison, Peter, Wes, Thora, and Mena. Most of that remains for you to see on film, but some of it is even here: Carolyn's dialogue with herself at the dinner table, Lester's phone conversation at work, and a variety of other improvisations that Alan shaped and positioned and now remain as a testament to the sheer pleasure we took in rehearsing and shooting this film.

But in the end, without Alan's work on the original script, none of these people, myself included, would have taken this particular journey. And as I sit writing this in the dry, odourless L.A. sunshine, contemplating my twelve months working on the movie and looking forward to going home, I can only reflect on the power of the written word to change our little lives.

DREAMWORKS PICTURES presents

A Jinks/Cohen Company Production

Kevin Spacey   Annette Bening

AMERICAN BEAUTY

Thora Birch   Wes Bentley   Mena Suvari

Peter Gallagher   Allison Janney   Scott Bakula

Sam Robards   and Chris Cooper

Directed by   Sam Mendes

Written by   Alan Ball

Produced by   Bruce Cohen & Dan Jinks

Director of Photography   Conrad L. Hall, A.S.C.

Production Designer   Naomi Shohan

Edited by   Tariq Anwar

Chris Greenbury

Casting by   Debra Zane, C.S.A.

Costume Designer   Julie Weiss

Music Supervisor   Chris Douridas

Co-Producers   Stan Wlodkowski

Alan Ball

Music by   Thomas Newman

CAST

Lester Burnham   Kevin Spacey

Carolyn Burnham   Annette Bening

Jane Burnham   Thora Birch

Ricky Fitts   Wes Bentley

Angela Hayes   Mena Suvari

Buddy Kane   Peter Gallagher

Barbara Fitts   Allison Janney

Colonel Fitts   Chris Cooper

Jim #1   Scott Bakula

Jim #2   Sam Robards

Brad   Barry Del Sherman

Sale House Woman #1   Ara Cell

Sale House Man #1   John Cho

Sale House Man #2   Fort Atkinson

Sale House Woman #2   Sue Casey

Sale House Man #3   Kent Faulcon

Sale House Women #4   Brenda Wehle

Lisa Cloud

Spartanette #1   Alison Faulk

Spartanette #2   Krista Goodsitt

Spartanette #3   Lily Houtkin

Spartanette #4   Carolina Lancaster

Spartanette #5   Romana Leah

Spartanette #6   Chekesa Van Putten

Spartanette #7   Emily Zachary

Spartanette #8   Nancy Anderson

Unit Production Manager   Cristen Carr Strubbe

First Assistant Directors   Tony Adler

Carey Dietrich

Second Assistant Director   Rosemary Cremona

Choreographer   Paula Abdul

CREW

Art Director   David S. Lazan

Assistant Art Director   Catherine Smith

Set Decorator   Jan K. Bergstrom, S.D.S.A.

Camera Operator   Aaron Pazanti

First Assistant Camera   Clyde E. Bryan

Second Assistant Camera   Suzanne M. Trucks

Camera Loader   Michael Thomas

Still Photographer   Lorey Sebastian

Script Supervisor   Ana Maria Quintana

Supervising Sound Editor

Scott Martin Gershin, M.P.S.E.

Re-Recording Mixers   Scott Millan & Bob Beemer

Production Sound Mixer   Richard Van Dyke

Boom Operator   Carl Fisher

Video Camera Operator   Geoffrey Haley

Chief Lighting Technician   Tom Stern

Assistant Chief Lighting Technician   John Carney

Rigging Gaffer   Huston Beaumont

Electricians

Lester Boykin   Ross Dunkerley

Earl Gayer   John Lacy

David Neale   Andy Towne

Key Grip   Bill Young

Best Boy Grips   Don Vos

Dean King

Dolly Grip   Carlos Gallardo

Rigging Key Grip   Jerry King

Grips

Tom Boone   John Emory

Ron Glenn   Thomas Noroian

Property Master   Lynda Reiss

Assistant Property Master   Angela Whiting

Special Effects Coordinator   John C. Hartigan

Special Effects Assistants

Jason Hansen   Wayne Incorvaia

Gene Rizzardi   Paul Sokol

Michael Thompson   Christopher Walkowiak

Costume Supervisor   Hope B. Slepak

Assistant Costume Designer   Marcy Froehlich

Key Costumer   Sanford Slepak

Set Costumers   Alix Hester

Kanani Wolf

Key Makeup Artist   Tania McComas

Makeup Artist   Christine M. Steele

Ms. Bening's Makeup Artist   Julie Hewett

Key Hair Stylist   Carol A. O'Connell

Hair Stylist   Patricia Dehaney-Le May

Ms. Bening's Hair Stylist   Cydney Cornell

Production Coordinator   Christa Vausbinder

Assistant Production Coordinator

Shannon Speaker

Production Secretary   Matt Walker

Production Controller   Jim Turner

Production Accountant   Janet Lonsdale

Assistant Accountants   Tricia Kingery

Victor Haddox

Payroll Accountant   Debbie Lynn Siegel

Post Production Accountant   Maria DeVane

Location Manager   Christine Bonnem

Key Assistant Location Manager   Yoshi Enoki, Jr.

Locations Assistant   Chee Ho

Second Assistant Director   Peter E. Hirsch

Second Second Assistant Director

Stephanie Kime

Casting Assistant   Terri Taylor

Extras Casting   Raquel Osborne

Assistant Choreographer   Cindy Picker

Unit Publicist   David Linck

Art Department Coordinator   Molly Click

Set Decoration Coordinator   Lisa Penaranda

Set Designers   Andrea Dopaso

Suzan Wexler

Storyboard Artists   Robin Richesson

Tony Chance

Leadpersons   Michael P. Casey

Michael Higelmire

Swing Gang

Brook Bacon   Kevin Chambers

Gary Kudroff   John A. Scott III

On-Set Dressers   Carolyn Lassek

Ian Kay

Researcher   Deborah Ricketts

Construction Coordinator   Joe Ondrejko

Propmaker Foreman   Robert Garlow

Paint Foreman   Tom Hrupcho

Plasterer Foreman   Jim Heritage

Greens Foreman   Richard W. Jones

Standby Painter   Chris Zimmerman

Transportation Coordinator   A. Welch Lambeth

Transportation Captain   Randy Lovelady

Drivers

Jeff Couch	Ed Evans
Jim Johnson	Al Kaminsky
Ron Linxwiler	George R. Matejka
Hector Mendoza	Wayne Parviainen
Glen R. Polzel	Daniel Routhieaux
Paul Schwanke	Tyler Tennesen
Jon Thorgusen	Dave Trevino
Daniel Valenzuela	Bill Wolff
Prentis Woods	Mark Yacullo

Craft Service   Charles 'Billy' Weaver

Caterer   Deluxe

Animal Handler   Joy A. Green

Studio Teacher   Pia Mehr

24-Frame Video Playback $E=mc^2$

24-Frame Video Playback Technician

Jennifer Carlson

Assistant to Mr. Mendes   Tara B. Cook

Assistant to Mr. Cohen & Mr. Jinks   Kelly Stuart

Assistant to Ms. Bening   Kim Mozingo

Assistants to Mr. Spacey   Mike Welch

Dana Brunetti

Personal Trainer to Mr. Spacey   Mike Torchia

Production Assistants

Steven Buhai	Stephen P. Del Prete
Anna E. Hayward	Maurice 'Moe' Freeman
Jeffrey Jenofsky	Mark Rabinowitz
J. Ben Sykes	George L. Tarrant, Jr.
Christian Walsh	Gillian Martin Waterman

Stand-Ins

Marina Freeman	Nichole McWhorter
Damon Preston	Daniel J. Walsh

First Aid   Timothy J. Werle

Robert Brugger

Construction First Aid   Lance Mancuso

Post Production Executive   Martin Cohen

Post Production Supervisor   Lisa Dennis Kennedy

Post Production Coordinator   Lisa Marie Serra

First Assistant Editors   Tracey Wadmore-Smith

Larry Madaras

Avid Assistants   Vince Filippone

P.J. Harling

Editorial Production Assistant   Jeffrey Skinner

Projectionist   Rene Gonzales

First Assistant Sound Editor

Thomas O'Neil Younkman

ADR Supervisor   Trevor Jolly

Dialogue Editors   Simon Coke

Mark Gordon

Sound Effects Editors   Alan Rankin

Bryan Bowen

Foley Editors   Peter Zinda

Tom Ozanich

Digital Sound Assistants   Paul Flinchbaugh

Leo LeBaigue

ADR Mixers   Richard Weingart

Dean Drabin

ADR Recordist   Brian Basham

Foley Artists   Jeffrey B. Wilhoit

James Moriana

Foley Mixer   Nerses Gezalyan

Foley Recordist   Greg Zimmerman

Additional Audio   Mark Ormandy

ADR Voice Casting   L.A. MadDogs

Re-Recorded at   Todd-Ao West

Executive in Charge of Music   Todd Homme

Music Editors   Bill Bernstein

Joanie Diener

Assistant Music Editor   Jordan Corngold

Titles & Opticals   Pacific Title Research

Avid Equipment by   Des

Negative Cutter   Kona Cutting

Color Timer   Phil Heto

Camera Cranes & Dollies by

Chapman/Leonard Studio Equipment, Inc.

Second Unit

First Assistant Director   Chris Edmonds

Second Assistant Director

Michelle Muggs Edmonds

Directors of Photography   Conrad Hall, Jr.

David Golia

First Assistant Camera   David Riley

Second Assistant Camera   Mike Gentile

Script Supervisor   Marilyn Giardino-Zyeh

Visual Effects Gaffer   James McEwen

Chief Lighting Technician   James Cox

Assistant Chief Lighting Technician

Patrick Ralston

Key Grip   Kenny King

Best Boy Grip   Paul Farley

Dolly Grip   Sergio 'Ponch' Gutierrez

Set Costumer   Lee Harris

Makeup Artist   Juliet Loveland

Hair Stylists   Cheri Ruff

Steve R. Soussana

Technical Assistants   Jenny Behnke

Sheldon Ramones

David Durham

Nicolle Gray

Runner   John Bozzalla

Managing Director   Don Fly

Special thanks to Pete Townshend

Thanks to all at the Donmar Warehouse in London

Dr. Bill and Alice

Filmed at Warner Bros. Studios,

Burbank, California

Credits not final at time of publication

AMERICAN BEAUTY

Screenplay by Alan Ball

FADE IN:

INT. FITTS HOUSE – RICKY'S BEDROOM – NIGHT

>*On VIDEO: JANE BURNHAM lays in bed, wearing a tank top. She's sixteen, with dark, intense eyes.*

JANE   I need a father who's a role model, not some horny geek-boy who's gonna spray his shorts whenever I bring a girlfriend home from school.
(snorts)
What a lame-o. Somebody really should put him out of his misery.

>*Her mind wanders for a beat.*

RICKY *(O.C.)* Want me to kill him for you?

>*Jane looks at us and sits up.*

JANE *(deadpan)* Yeah, would you?

>*FADE TO BLACK.*

>*FADE IN:*

EXT. ROBIN HOOD TRAIL – EARLY MORNING

>*We're FLYING above suburban America, DESCENDING SLOWLY toward a tree-lined street.*

LESTER *(V.O.)* My name is Lester Burnham. This is my
neighborhood. This is my street. This... is my life.
I'm forty-two years old. In less than a year,
I'll be dead.

INT. BURNHAM HOUSE – MASTER BEDROOM
– CONTINUOUS

*We're looking down at a king-sized BED from
OVERHEAD: LESTER BURNHAM lies sleeping
amidst expensive bed linens, face down, wearing
PAJAMAS. An irritating ALARM CLOCK RINGS.
Lester gropes blindly to shut it off.*

LESTER *(V.O.)* Of course, I don't know that yet.

*He rolls over, looks up at us and sighs. He doesn't
seem too thrilled at the prospect of a new day.*

LESTER *(V.O.)* And in a way, I'm dead already.

He sits up and puts on his slippers.

INT. BURNHAM HOUSE – MASTER BATH
– MOMENTS LATER

*Lester thrusts his face directly into a steaming
hot shower. ANGLE from outside the shower:
Lester's naked body is silhouetted through the*

fogged-up glass door. It becomes apparent
he is masturbating.

LESTER *(V.O) (amused)* Look at me, jerking off in the
shower.
(then)
This will be the high point of my day. It's all
downhill from here.

EXT. BURNHAM HOUSE – MOMENTS LATER

CLOSE on a single, dewy AMERICAN BEAUTY
ROSE. A gloved hand with CLIPPERS appears
and SNIPS the flower off.

CAROLYN BURNHAM tends her rose bushes in
front of the Burnham house. A very well-put
together woman of forty, she wears colour-co-
ordinated gardening togs and has lots of useful
and expensive tools.

Lester watches her through a WINDOW on the
first floor, peeping out through the drapes.

LESTER *(V.O.)* That's my wife Carolyn. See the way the
handle on those pruning shears matches her
gardening clogs? That's not an accident.

EXT. JIMS' HOUSE – CONTINUOUS

> In the fenced front yard of the house next door, a dog BARKS repeatedly. A MAN in a conservative suit (JIM #1) chastises the barking dog.

JIM #1   Hush, Bitsy. You hush. What is wrong?

LESTER *(V.O.)* That's our next-door neighbour Jim.

> A second MAN in a conservative suit (JIM #2) comes out of the house.

LESTER *(V.O.)* And that's his lover, Jim.

JIM #2 *(re: barking dog)* What in the world is wrong with her? She had a walk this morning.

JIM #1   And a jerky treat.

JIM #2   You spoil her.
            (sternly)
            Bitsy. No bark. Come inside. Now.

EXT. BURNHAM HOUSE – CONTINUOUS

> Lester watches all this from the window.

CAROLYN Good morning, Jim!

4

> *Jim #1 walks toward the fence to greet Carolyn.*

JIM #1   Morning, Carolyn.

CAROLYN *(overly friendly)* I just love your tie! That colour!

JIM #1   I just love your roses. How do you get them to
          flourish like this?

CAROLYN Well, I'll tell you. Egg shells and Miracle Grow.

> *Jim #1 and Carolyn continue to chat, unaware
> that Lester is watching them.*

LESTER *(V.O.)* Man. I get exhausted just watching her.

> *Lester's POV: We can't hear what Jim and
> Carolyn are saying, but she's overly animated,
> like a TV talk show host.*

LESTER *(V.O.)* She wasn't always like this. She used to be
          happy. *We* used to be happy.

**INT. BURNHAM HOUSE – JANE'S ROOM
– CONTINUOUS**

> *JANE is seated at her desk, working at her
> computer.*

LESTER *(V.O.)* My daughter Jane. Only child.

CLOSE on the COMPUTER MONITOR: A PERSONAL BANKING SOFTWARE window suddenly disappears to reveal another window: a PLASTIC SURGERY WEB SITE, featuring clinical 'before' and 'after' photos of surgically augmented breasts.

LESTER *(V.O.)* Janie's a pretty typical teenager. Angry, insecure, confused. I wish I could tell her that's all going to pass...

Outside, a CAR HORN BLARES. Jane stuffs items into her BACKPACK.

LESTER *(V.O.)* But I don't want to lie to her.

We HEAR the CAR HORN again from outside. Jane studies herself in a mirror, then shifts to get a good profile of her breasts.

EXT. BURNHAM HOUSE – CONTINUOUS

Carolyn stands next to a platinum-colored MERCEDES-BENZ ML320, reaching in through the drivers' window to blow the HORN again.

Jane shuffles out of the house, her backpack slung over her shoulder.

CAROLYN Jane. Honey. Are you trying to look unattractive?

JANE   Yes.

CAROLYN Well, congratulations. You've succeeded
         admirably.

         *Jane gets in the car. Lester hurries out the front
         door, carrying a BRIEFCASE.*

CAROLYN Lester, could you make me a little later, please?
         Because I'm not quite late enough.

         *Lester's briefcase suddenly springs open and his
         papers spill all over the driveway. He drops to his
         knees to gather everything.*

JANE   Nice going, Dad.

         *Lester smiles sheepishly, trying to lighten the
         moment.*

         *His POV: Carolyn looks down at us,
         contemptuous but also bored, as if she gave up
         expecting anything more long ago.*

LESTER *(V.O.)* Both my wife and daughter think I'm this
         gigantic loser, and... they're right.

INT. MERCEDES-BENZ ML320
– A SHORT TIME LATER

> *Carolyn is driving; Jane stares out the window.*
> *Lester is asleep in the back seat.*

LESTER *(V.O.)* I have lost something. I'm not exactly sure
what it is, but I know I didn't always feel this...
sedated. But you know what? It's never too late
to get it back.

INT. OFFICE BUILDING – DAY

> *Lester sits at his workstation, a BEIGE CUBICLE*
> *surrounded by IDENTICAL BEIGE CUBICLES.*
> *He's staring at a computer monitor and talking on*
> *a HEADSET PHONE. The beleaguered expression*
> *on his face is at odds with the light, friendly tone*
> *of his voice.*

LESTER Hello, this is Lester Burnham from *Media Monthly*
magazine, I'm calling for Mr. Tamblin, please?...
Well, we're all under a deadline here, uh, but you
see, there is some basic information about the
product launch that isn't even covered in your
press release and I... Yeah. Can I ask you a
question? Who is Tamblin? Does he exist?
'Cause he doesn't ever seem to come in...
Yeah, okay, I'll leave my number...

> *BRAD, a dapper man in his thirties, approaches and observes Lester, who is unaware of his presence.*

LESTER   It's 555 0199. Lester Burnham. Thank you!

> *Lester disconnects the call, obviously irritated.*

BRAD   Hey Les. You got a minute?

> *Lester turns around, smiling perfunctorily*

LESTER   For you, Brad? I've got five.

INT. BRAD'S OFFICE – MOMENTS LATER

> *Brad is seated behind his desk in his big corner office.*

BRAD   I'm sure you can understand our need to cut corners around here.

> *Lester sits across from him, looking small and isolated.*

LESTER   Oh, sure. Times are tight, and you gotta free up cash. Gotta spend money to make money. Right?

BRAD   Exactly. So...

Brad stands, ready to usher Lester out.

LESTER *(blurts)* Like the time when Mr. Flournoy used the company MasterCard to pay for that hooker, and then she used the card numbers and stayed at the St. Regis for, what was it, like, three months?

BRAD *(startled)* That's unsubstantiated gossip.

LESTER That's fifty thousand dollars. That's somebody's salary. That's somebody who's gonna get fired because Craig has to pay women to fuck him!

BRAD Jesus. Calm down. Nobody's getting fired yet. That's why we're having everyone write out a job description, mapping out in detail how they contribute. That way, management can assess who's valuable and—

LESTER Who's expendable.

BRAD It's just business.

LESTER *(angry)* I've been writing for this magazine for fourteen years, Brad. You've been here how long, a whole month?

BRAD *(frank)* I'm one of the good guys, Les. I'm trying to level with you. This is your one chance to save your job.

Lester stares at him, powerless.

EXT. BURNHAM HOUSE – LATE AFTERNOON

> *A MOVING VAN is parked in front of the*
> *COLONIAL HOUSE next door to the Burnhams'.*
> *Movers carry furniture toward the house.*
> *The Mercedes-Benz pulls into the Burnham*
> *driveway. Carolyn drives, Lester is in the*
> *passenger seat.*

CAROLYN —there is no decision, you just write the damn
thing!

LESTER You don't think it's weird and kinda fascist?

CAROLYN Possibly. But you don't want to be unemployed.

LESTER Oh, well, let's just all sell our souls and work for
Satan, because it's more convenient that way.

CAROLYN Could you be just a little bit more dramatic,
please, huh?

> *As they get out of the car, Carolyn scopes out the*
> *MOVERS next door.*

CAROLYN So we've finally got new neighbors. You know,
if the Lomans had let *me* represent them,
instead of –
(heavy disdain)
– 'The Real Estate King,' that house would never
have sat on the market for six months.

She heads into the house, followed by Lester.

LESTER   Well, they were still mad at you for cutting down their sycamore.

CAROLYN   *Their* sycamore? C'mon! A substantial portion of the root structure was on our property. You know that. How can you call it their sycamore? I wouldn't have the heart to just cut down something if it wasn't partially mine, which of course it was.

INT. BURNHAM HOUSE – DINING ROOM
– LATER THAT NIGHT

We HEAR EASY-LISTENING MUSIC. Lester, Carolyn and Jane are eating dinner by CANDLELIGHT. RED ROSES are bunched in a vase at the center of the table. Nobody makes eye contact, or even seems aware of anybody else's presence, until...

JANE   Mom, do we always have to listen to this elevator music?

CAROLYN   *(considers)* No. No, we don't. As soon as you've prepared a nutritious yet savoury meal that *I'm* about to eat, you can listen to whatever you like.

A long beat. Lester suddenly turns to Jane.

LESTER   So Janie, how was school?

JANE   *(suspicious)* It was okay.

LESTER   Just okay?

JANE   No, Dad. It was spec-tac-ular.

    A beat.

LESTER   Well, you want to know how things went at my
    job today?

    Now she looks at him as if he's lost his mind.

LESTER   They've hired this efficiency expert, this really
    friendly guy named Brad, how perfect is that?
    And he's basically there to make it seem like
    they're justified in firing somebody, because they
    couldn't just come right out and say that, could
    they? No, no, that would be too... honest.
    And so they've asked us—
    (off her look)
    —you couldn't possibly care any less, could you?

    Carolyn is watching this closely.

JANE   *(uncomfortable)* Well, what do you expect? You can't
    all of a sudden be my best friend, just because
    you had a bad day.

She gets up and heads toward the kitchen.

JANE   I mean, hello. You've barely even spoken to me
        for months.

        *She's gone. Lester notices Carolyn looking
        at him critically.*

LESTER Oh, what, you're mother-of-the-year? You treat
        her like an employee.

CAROLYN (taken aback) What?!

        Lester is quiet, staring at his plate.

CAROLYN *(more authority)* What?

        *Lester gets up and starts after Jane, taking his
        plate with him.*

LESTER I'm going to get some ice cream.

        Carolyn watches him go, irritated.

INT. BURNHAM HOUSE – CONTINUOUS

        *Jane stands at the sink, rinsing off her plate.
        Lester enters.*

LESTER Honey, I'm sorry. I...

> *Jane turns and stares at him, waiting for him to finish.*

LESTER   I'm sorry I haven't been more available, I just... I'm...

> *He's looking to her for a little help here, but she's too uncomfortable with this sudden intimacy to give him any.*

LESTER   (finally) You know, you don't always have to wait for me to come to *you*...

JANE   Oh, great. So now it's my fault?

LESTER   I didn't say that. It's nobody's fault. Janie, what happened? You and I used to be pals.

EXT. BURNHAM HOUSE – CONTINUOUS

> *On VIDEO: We're looking through GREENHOUSE WINDOWS at Lester and Jane in the kitchen . We can't hear what they're saying, but it's obvious it's not going well. Jane puts her plate in the dishwasher and leaves. We FOLLOW HER out the door, then the camera JERKS back to Lester calling after her.*

> *CLOSE on the face of RICKY FITTS, illuminated by the screen of his DIGICAM as he videotapes.*

Ricky is eighteen, but his eyes are much older. Beneath his Zen-like tranquility lurks something wounded... and dangerous.

His POV, on VIDEO: Through the kitchen window, we see Lester at the sink, rinsing off his plate, muttering to himself. His head suddenly jerks up and he looks at us, as if he realizes he's being watched.

INT. BURNHAM HOUSE – KITCHEN – CONTINUOUS

Lester's POV: We're looking out through the kitchen window at the point where Ricky was just standing, but he's no longer there. Lester turns off the tap, dries his hands, then tosses the towel on the counter on his way out, where it lands next to a framed PHOTOGRAPH of Lester, Carolyn, and a much-younger Jane, taken several years earlier at an amusement park. It's startling how happy they look.

EXT. SALE HOUSE – DAY

CLOSE on a wooden SIGN that reads:
OPEN HOUSE TODAY
BURNHAM & ASSOCIATES REALTY
555-0195 Carolyn Burnham

The sign is planted in front of a RUN-DOWN HOME in a run-down neighborhood. The Mercedes is parked in front of the house. Carolyn, wearing a smart business suit, is unloading a box of cleaning supplies and a BOOMBOX from the back of the Mercedes when something across the street catches her eye.

Her POV: In front of a different house with much more curb appeal is another SIGN, featuring a picture of a handsome silver-haired MAN. It reads: Another One SOLD By Buddy Kane The Real Estate King 555-0100

Carolyn frowns and slams the back of the Mercedes shut.

INT. SALE HOUSE – LIVING ROOM – MOMENTS LATER

The interior of this house is ugly, oppressive and tasteless. Carolyn opens the front door, breathes deeply and solemnly announces:

CAROLYN I will sell this house today.

She neatly arranges her sales materials on a desk, then strips down to her undergarments.

MONTAGE:

> *We see Carolyn, working with fierce concentration as she: cleans glass doors that overlook the patio and pool; doggedly scrubs countertops in the kitchen; perches on a stepladder to dust a cheap-looking ceiling fan in the master bedroom; and vacuums a dirty carpet that will never be clean. Throughout all this, she keeps repeating to herself:*

CAROLYN I will sell this house today.
I will sell this house today.
I will sell this house today.

INT. SALE HOUSE – BATHROOM – LATER

> *Carolyn stands in front of the mirror, wearing her suit once more, applying lipstick. She stares at her reflection critically.*

CAROLYN I will sell this house today.

> *She says this as if it were a threat, then notices a smudge on the mirror and wipes it off.*

EXT. SALE HOUSE – FRONT YARD – LATER

> *The front door opens to reveal Carolyn,*
> *greeting us with the smile she thinks could*
> *sell ice to an Eskimo.*

CAROLYN Welcome. I'm Carolyn Burnham!

INT. SALE HOUSE – FOYER – CONTINUOUS

> *Smiling, Carolyn leads a man and woman into the*
> *living room. They're thirtyish, and they've seen a*
> *lot of houses today.*

CAROLYN This living room is very dramatic. Wait 'til you
see the native stone fireplace!

> *The man and woman glance around the dark*
> *room, unimpressed.*

CAROLYN A simple cream would really lighten things up.
You could even put in a skylight.

> *The woman wrinkles her face, skeptical.*

CAROLYN Well, why don't we go into the kitchen?

INT. SALE HOUSE – KITCHEN – LATER

> *Carolyn enters, followed by a different couple in their fifties.*

CAROLYN It's a dream come true for any cook. Just filled with positive energy. Huh?

INT. SALE HOUSE – MASTER BEDROOM – LATER

> *Carolyn stands with a different couple: African American, late twenties. The woman is pregnant.*

CAROLYN ...and you'll be surprised how much a ceiling fan can cut down on your energy costs.

EXT. SALE HOUSE – BACK YARD – LATER

> *Carolyn stands by the pool next to two fortyish WOMEN.*

CAROLYN You know, you could have some really fun backyard get-togethers out here.

WOMAN #1 The ad said this pool was 'lagoon-like.' There's nothing 'lagoon-like' about it. Except for maybe the bugs.

WOMAN #2 There's not even any plants out here.

CAROLYN *(re: shrub)* What do you call this? Is this not a plant? If you have a problem with the plants, I can always call my landscape architect. Solved.

WOMAN #2 I mean, I think 'lagoon,' I think waterfall, I think tropical. This is a cement hole.

A beat.

CAROLYN I have some tiki torches in the garage.

INT. SALE HOUSE – SUN ROOM – LATER

> *Carolyn enters, alone. She's furious. She locks the sliding glass door and starts to pull the vertical blinds shut, then stops. Standing very still, with the blinds casting shadows across her face, she starts to cry: brief, staccato SOBS that seemingly escape against her will. Suddenly she SLAPS herself, hard.*

CAROLYN Shut up. Stop it. You... Weak!

> *But the tears continue. She SLAPS herself again.*

CAROLYN Weak. Baby. Shut up. Shut up! Shut up!

> *She SLAPS herself repeatedly until she stops crying. She stands there, taking deep breaths until she has everything under control, then pulls*

the blinds shut, once again all business. She
walks out calmly, leaving us alone in the dark,
empty room. We HEAR CHEERING and
APPLAUSE.

INT. HIGH SCHOOL GYMNASIUM – NIGHT

We're at a high-school BASKETBALL GAME.
Teenage boys play a fast and furious game.
One team wearing pale blue and white uniforms
scores a basket. Perky cheerleaders jump up and
down as the CROWD goes wild. Seated in the
bleachers, next to the high school BAND, is a
group of about twenty TEENAGE GIRLS, dressed
in pale blue and white uniforms. Among them,
Jane sits next to ANGELA HAYES. At sixteen,
Angela is strikingly beautiful; with perfect even
features, blonde hair and a nubile young body,
she's the archetypal American dream girl.
Jane stands and scans the bleachers.

ANGELA   Who are you looking for?

JANE   My parents are coming tonight. They're trying to,
you know, take an active interest in me.

ANGELA   Gross. I hate it when my mom does that.

JANE   They're such assholes. Why can't they just have
their own lives?

INT. MERCEDES-BENZ ML320 – CONTINUOUS

Carolyn drives. Lester is slumped in the passenger seat.

LESTER What makes you so sure she wants us to be there? Did she ask us to come?

CAROLYN Of course not. She doesn't want us to know how important this is to her. But she's been practicing her steps for weeks.

LESTER Well, I bet money she's going to resent it. And I'm missing the James Bond marathon on TNT.

CAROLYN Lester, this is important. I'm sensing a real distance growing between you and Jane.

LESTER Growing? She hates me.

CAROLYN She's just willful.

LESTER She hates you too.

Carolyn stares at him, unsure of how to respond.

INT. HIGH SCHOOL GYMNASIUM – LATER

The uniformed girls now stand in formation on the gym floor.

ANNOUNCER *(over P.A.)* And now, for your half-time entertainment, Rockwell High's award-winning Dancing Spartanettes!

In the crowded stands, Lester and Carolyn find seats.

LESTER We can leave right after this, right?

The HIGH SCHOOL BAND plays 'ON BROADWAY.' On the gym floor, the girls perform. They're well-rehearsed, but too young to carry off the ambitious Vegas routine they're attempting. Lester, watching from the stands, picks out his daughter.

His POV: Jane performs well, concentrating. Dancing awkwardly next to her is Angela. Suddenly Angela looks right at us and smiles... a lazy, insolent smile. Lester leans forward in his seat.

His POV: We're focused on Angela now. Everything starts to SLOW DOWN... the MUSIC acquires an eerie ECHO... We ZOOM slowly toward Lester as he watches, transfixed. His POV: Angela's awkwardness gives way to a fluid grace, and 'ON BROADWAY' FADES into dreamy, hypnotic MUSIC. The light on Angela grows stronger, and the other girls DISAPPEAR entirely. Lester is suddenly alone in the stands, spellbound.

His POV: Angela looks directly at us now, dancing only for Lester. Her movements take on a blatantly erotic edge as she starts to unzip her uniform, teasing us with an expression that's both innocent and knowing, then... she pulls her uniform OPEN and a profusion of RED ROSE PETALS spill forth... and we SMASH CUT TO:

INT. HIGH SCHOOL GYMNASIUM – CONTINUOUS

Angela, fully clothed, is once again surrounded by the other girls. The HIGH SCHOOL BAND plays its last note, the Dancing Spartanettes strike their final pose, and the audience APPLAUDS. Carolyn claps along with the rest of the audience. Lester just sits there, unable to take his eyes off Angela.

EXT. HIGH SCHOOL GYMNASIUM – LATER

The game is long over. Jane and Angela come out of the gym.

JANE   Oh shit, they're still here.

Her POV: Lester and Carolyn stand at the edge of the parking lot.

LESTER   Janie!

CAROLYN Hi! I really enjoyed that!

> *She crosses reluctantly toward her parents,*
> *followed by Angela.*

LESTER Congratulations, honey, you were great.

JANE I didn't win anything.

LESTER *(to Angela)* Hi, I'm Lester. Janie's dad.

ANGELA Oh. Hi.

> *An awkward beat.*

JANE This is my friend, Angela Hayes.

LESTER Okay, good to meet you. You were also good
        tonight. Very... precise.

ANGELA *(warming)* Thanks.

CAROLYN *(to Angela)* Nice to meet you, Angela.
        (to Jane) Honey, I'm so proud of you. I watched
        you very closely, and you didn't screw up once.
        (then, to Lester) Okay, we have to go.

> *She starts toward the parking lot.*
> *Lester stays behind.*

LESTER So, what are you girls doing now?

JANE   Dad.

ANGELA   We're going out for pizza.

LESTER   Oh really, do you need a ride? We can give you a
          ride. I have a car. You wanna come with us?

ANGELA   Thanks... but I have a car.

LESTER   Oh, you have a car. Oh. That's great! That's great,
          because Janie's thinking about getting a car soon
          too, aren't you, honey?

JANE *(you freak)* Dad. Mom's waiting for you.

LESTER   Well, it was very nice meeting you, Angela.
          Any, uh, friend of Janie's is a friend of mine.

          *Angela smiles, aware of the power she has over
          him. He is mesmerized; grateful, even.*

LESTER   Well... I'll be seeing you around then.

          Lester waves awkwardly as he crosses off.

JANE   Could he be any more pathetic?

ANGELA   I think it's sweet. And I think he and your mother
          have not had sex in a long time.

INT. BURNHAM HOUSE – MASTER BEDROOM – A FEW HOURS LATER

> CLOSE on a solitary red ROSE PETAL as it
> falls slowly through the air. We're looking down
> on Lester and Carolyn in bed. Even in sleep,
> Carolyn looks determined. Lester is awake and
> stares up at us.

LESTER *(V.O.)* It's the weirdest thing.

> The ROSE PETAL drifts into view, landing
> on his pillow.

LESTER *(V.O.)* I feel like I've been in a coma for about
twenty years, and I'm just now waking up.

> More ROSE PETALS fall onto the bed, and he
> smiles up at...

> His POV: Angela, naked, FLOATS above us as a
> deluge of ROSE PETALS falls around her. Her hair
> fans out around her head and GLOWS with a
> subtle, burnished light. She looks down at us with
> a smile that is all things... Lester smiles back and
> LAUGHS, as ROSE PETALS cover his face.

LESTER *(V.O.)* Spec-tac-ular.

EXT. ROBIN HOOD TRAIL – CONTINUOUS

A WHITE BMW 328si CONVERTIBLE is parked on the street outside the Burnham's house. We HEAR girlish LAUGHTER from inside.

INT. ANGELA'S BMW – CONTINUOUS

Angela is behind the wheel, Jane in the passenger seat. They're passing a JOINT back and forth.

JANE   I'm sorry my dad was so weird tonight.

ANGELA   It's okay. I'm used to guys drooling over me. It started when I was about twelve, I'd go out to dinner with my parents. Every Thursday night, Red Lobster. And every guy there would stare at me when I walked in. And I knew what they were thinking. Just like I knew guys at school thought about me when they jerked off.

JANE   Vomit.

ANGELA   No, I liked it. And I still like it. If people I don't even know look at me and want to fuck me, it means I really have a shot at being a model. Which is great, because there's nothing worse in life than being ordinary.

> *An awkward beat. Jane stares at the floor.*

JANE   I really think it'll happen for you.

ANGELA Oh, I know. Because everything that was meant
        to happen, does. Eventually.

EXT. BURNHAM HOUSE – CONTINUOUS

> *On VIDEO: Jane gets out of the car, still
> LAUGHING, and waves as Angela pulls away.
> We ZOOM toward Jane as she walks up the
> driveway. She turns suddenly, sensing our
> presence.*

> *Her POV: We're looking at the COLONIAL
> HOUSE next door where the moving van was
> parked earlier. The front porch is shrouded in
> darkness... then a PORCH LIGHT abruptly reveals
> Ricky. As usual, he's dressed conservatively.
> There is a BEEPER attached to his belt, and his
> DIGICAM dangles loosely around his neck.
> Irritated, Jane stares at him, hard.*

JANE   Asshole.

> *He looks back at her curiously, then raises his
> Digicam and starts to videotape her.*

His POV, on VIDEO: Jane, angry and self-conscious, turns and walks quickly toward her house, flipping us off as she goes.

INT. BURNHAM HOUSE – FOYER – CONTINUOUS

Jane enters, closes and locks the door. She quickly *TURNS OFF THE LIGHT* that's been left on for her, then peeks through a window.

Her POV: There's no sign of Ricky.
Jane turns back into the room, her heart racing... and smiles.

INT. BURNHAM HOUSE – JANE'S BEDROOM – THE NEXT MORNING

CLOSE on an *ADDRESS BOOK:* A man's hand flips to the H page and then his finger stops at the name Angela Hayes. Lester, dressed for work, goes through Jane's address book. We *HEAR* the *SHOWER* running in the adjacent bathroom. He grabs Jane's phone and dials, then stands with the receiver to his ear, nervous.

ANGELA *(over phone line)* Hello? Hello?

Lester is frozen, unable to speak. Suddenly, the *SHOWER* is turned off in the next room. Lester

> *hangs up and exits quickly. A moment, then the*
> *PHONE RINGS. Jane emerges from the*
> *bathroom, a towel wrapped around her torso,*
> *drying her wet hair. She picks up the PHONE.*

JANE   Hello?

INT. HAYES HOUSE – ANGELA'S BEDROOM – CONTINUOUS

> *Angela is sprawled across her bed, on the phone.*

ANGELA   Why'd you call me?

INTERCUT WITH JANE IN HER BEDROOM:

JANE   I didn't.

ANGELA   Well, my phone just rang and I answered it and
            somebody hung up and then I star sixty-nined
            and it called you back.

JANE   I was in the shower.

> *Then Jane notices her address book open to the*
> *H page.*

JANE   Oh, gross.

32

EXT. BURNHAM HOUSE – CONTINUOUS

>   *On VIDEO: We're across from Jane's WINDOW, looking in. Jane picks up the address book, frowning. She speaks into the phone, but we can't hear her.*

WOMAN'S VOICE *(O.C.) (sing song)* Rick-y! Break-fast!

INT. FITTS HOUSE – RICKY'S BEDROOM – CONTINUOUS

>   *Ricky stands at his window, videotaping. He lowers his Digicam, but his eyes remain locked on Jane across the way.*

RICKY   Be right there.

INT. FITTS HOUSE – KITCHEN – MOMENTS LATER

>   *BARBARA FITTS stands at the stove, flipping bacon strips mechanically, her eyes focused elsewhere. At least ten years younger than her husband, she's pretty in a June Cleaver-ish way. The Colonel sits at a dinette reading* The Wall Street Journal. *Ricky enters.*

RICKY   Mom.

Startled, Barbara turns to him.

BARBARA Hello.

As she attempts to serve him bacon:

RICKY   I don't eat bacon, remember?

BARBARA (unnerved) I'm sorry, I must have forgotten.

*Ricky serves himself scrambled eggs from
another pan, then joins his father at the table.*

RICKY   What's new in the world, Dad?

COLONEL This country is going straight to hell.

*A DOORBELL rings. The Colonel and Barbara
look at each other, alarmed.*

COLONEL Are you expecting anyone?

BARBARA No. *(thinks)* No.

*The Colonel heads toward the living room, a little
puffed up.*

INT. FITTS HOUSE – FOYER – MOMENTS LATER

> The Colonel opens the front door to reveal the
> two JIMS.

JIM #1   Hi.

JIM #2   Welcome to the neighborhood.

> Jim #1 holds out a basket filled with flowers,
> vegetables and a small white cardboard box tied
> with raffia.

JIM #1   Just a little something from our garden.

JIM #2   Except for the pasta, we got that at Fallaci's.

JIM #1   It's unbelievably fresh. You just drop it in the
          water and it's done.

> The Colonel stares at them, suspicious.

JIM #1   *(offers his hand)* Jim Olmeyer. Two doors down.
          Welcome to the neighborhood.

COLONEL   *(shakes)* Colonel Frank Fitts, U.S. Marine Corps.

JIM #1   Nice to meet you. And this is my partner...

JIM #2   *(offers his hand)* Jim Berkley, but people call me J.B.

COLONEL Let's cut to the chase, okay? What are you guys
         selling?

JIM #2 *(after a beat)* Nothing. We just wanted to say hi to
         our new neighbours—

COLONEL Yeah, yeah, yeah. But you said you're partners.
         So what's your business?

         The Jims look at each other, then back at the
         Colonel.

JIM #1 Well, he's a tax attorney.

JIM #2 And he's an anaesthesiologist.

         The Colonel looks at them, confused.
         Then it dawns on him.

INT. COLONEL'S FORD EXPLORER – LATER

         The Colonel drives, staring darkly at the road
         ahead. In the passenger seat, Ricky is using a
         CALCULATOR and jotting numbers down in a
         NOTEBOOK.

COLONEL How come these faggots always have to rub it in
         your face? How can they be so shameless?

RICKY   That's the whole thing, Dad. They don't feel like
         it's anything to be ashamed of.

         The Colonel looks at Ricky sharply.

COLONEL Well, it is.

         *A beat, as Ricky continues his calculations, before
         he realizes a response is expected from him.
         Then:*

RICKY   Yeah, you're right.

         The Colonel's eyes flash angrily.

COLONEL Don't placate me like I'm your mother, boy.

         Ricky sighs, then looks at his father.

RICKY   Forgive me, sir, for speaking so bluntly, but those
         fags make me want to puke my fucking guts out.

         The Colonel is taken aback but quickly covers.

COLONEL Me too, son. Me too.

         *Case closed, Ricky goes back to his calculations.
         CLOSE on the pencil in his hands: He's totaling
         two columns of NUMBERS. Under the column
         'Income' he writes in swift, bold strokes:
         $24,950.00.*

EXT. HIGH SCHOOL CAMPUS – A SHORT TIME LATER

> *Jane and Angela are standing with two other*
> *TEENAGE GIRLS.*

ANGELA   I'm serious, he just pulled down his pants and yanked it out. You know, like, say hello to Mr. Happy.

TEENAGE GIRL #1   Gross.

ANGELA   It wasn't gross. It was kind of cool.

TEENAGE GIRL #1   So, did you do it with him?

ANGELA   Of course I did. He is a really well-known photographer? He shoots for *Elle* on like, a regular basis? It would have been so majorly stupid of me to turn him down.

TEENAGE GIRL #2   You are a total prostitute.

ANGELA   Hey. That's how things really are. You just don't know, because you're this pampered little suburban chick.

TEENAGE GIRL #2   So are you. You've only been in *Seventeen* once, and you looked fat, so stop acting like you're goddamn Christy Turlington.

*The two TEENAGE GIRLS move away from Jane
and Angela.*

ANGELA *(calling off)* Cunt!
        (then)
        I am so sick of people taking their insecurities out
        on me.

        *The Colonel's Ford Explorer pulls up, and Ricky
        gets out.*

JANE   Oh my God. That's the pervert who filmed me last
        night.

ANGELA Him? Jane. No way. He's a total lunatic.

JANE   You know him?

ANGELA Yeah. We were on the same lunch shift when I
        was in ninth grade, and he would always say the
        most random, weird things, and then one day, he
        was just like, gone. And then, Connie Cardullo
        told me he his parents had to put him in a mental
        institution.

JANE   Why? What did he do?

ANGELA What do you mean?

JANE   Well, they can't put you away just for saying
        weird things.

Angela stares at Jane, then her mouth widens into a smile.

ANGELA   You total slut. You've got a crush on him.

JANE   What? Please.

ANGELA   You were defending him! You love him. You want to have like, ten thousand of his babies.

JANE   Shut up.

Jane suddenly finds Ricky standing in front of her.

RICKY   Hi. My name's Ricky. I just moved next door to you.

JANE   I know. I kinda remember this really creepy incident when you were filming me last night?

RICKY   I didn't mean to scare you. I just think you're interesting.

Angela shoots a wide-eyed look at Jane, who ignores it.

JANE   Thanks, but I really don't need to have some psycho obsessing about me right now.

RICKY   I'm not obsessing. I'm just curious.

> *He looks at her intently, his eyes searching hers.*
> *Jane is unnerved and has to look away. Ricky*
> *smiles and walks off.*

ANGELA   What a freak. And why does he dress like a
         Bible salesman?

JANE   He's like, so confident. That can't be real.

ANGELA   I don't believe him. I mean, he didn't even like,
         look at me once.

INT. FITTS HOUSE – DEN – THAT NIGHT

> *CLOSE on a TV SCREEN:* Hogan's Heroes *on*
> Nick at Nite. *The Colonel and Barbara are seated*
> *on a couch, watching television. The Colonel is*
> *smiling, enjoying the show; Barbara just stares.*
> *The Colonel CHUCKLES at a joke and startles*
> *her. We HEAR a door opening elsewhere in the*
> *house, and Ricky enters.*

RICKY   Hey.

> *He sits on the couch, next to his father, and*
> *watches TV along with them. The Colonel's smile*
> *fades.*

BARBARA *(out of the blue)* I'm sorry, what?

RICKY   Mom. Nobody said anything.

BARBARA   Oh. I'm sorry.

          The three of them stare at the TV, like strangers in
          an airport.

INT. HOTEL BALLROOM – NIGHT

          We HEAR MUSIC under a room full of people all
          talking at once, as Lester and Carolyn enter a
          hotel ballroom. We FOLLOW THEM as they pass
          a SIGN that reads: GREATER ROCKWELL
          REALTOR RESOURCES GROUP

CAROLYN   —everyone here is with their spouse or their
          significant other. How would it look if I showed up
          with no one?

LESTER   Well, you always end up ignoring me and going
          off—

          Inside the ballroom, well-dressed real estate
          professionals stand in clumps, chatting. Catering
          waiters serve hors d'oeuvres.

CAROLYN   Now listen to me. This is an important business
          function. As you know, my business is selling an
          image. And part of my job is to *live* that image—

LESTER   Just say whatever you want to say and spare me
          the propaganda.

CAROLYN   *(spots someone)* Hi, Shirley!
          (to Lester)
          Listen, just do me a favor. Act happy tonight?

LESTER   *(grins stupidly)* I *am* happy, honey.

          Carolyn's jaw tightens, then:

CAROLYN   *(spots someone)* Oh! Buddy!

          *She drags Lester toward a silver-haired MAN and
          his much younger WIFE. We recognize the Man
          as BUDDY KANE, The Real Estate King.*

CAROLYN   *(shakes Buddy's hand)* Buddy! Buddy. Hi! Good
          to see you again.

BUDDY   It's so good to see you too, Catherine.

CAROLYN   Carolyn.

BUDDY   Carolyn! Of course. How are you?

CAROLYN   Very well, thank you.
          (to his wife)
          Hello, Christy.

CHRISTY   Hello.

CAROLYN My husband, Lester—

BUDDY *(shakes Lester's hand)* It's a pleasure.

LESTER Oh, we've met before, actually. This thing last
year. Or the Christmas thing at the Sheraton.

BUDDY Oh, yes.

LESTER It's okay. I wouldn't remember me either.

*He LAUGHS. A little too loudly. Carolyn
quickly joins in.*

CAROLYN *(forced gaiety)* Honey. Don't be weird.

*She smiles her most winning smile at him. He
knows this persona well, only it's never pissed
him off as much as it does right now.*

LESTER All right, honey. I won't be weird.
(his face close to hers)
I'll be whatever you want me to be.

*And he kisses her—a soft, warm kiss that speaks
unmistakably of sex—then turns to the others and
grins.*

LESTER We have a very healthy relationship.

BUDDY I see.

Carolyn's smile is frozen on her face.

LESTER   Well. I don't know about you, but I need a drink.

He crosses off. Carolyn, Buddy and Christy watch him go.

INT. HOTEL BALLROOM – MOMENTS LATER

Lester stands at the bar. A bartender pours him a drink.

LESTER   Whoa. Put a little more in there, cowboy.

The bartender complies. Lester takes his drink and turns to face the center of the room.

His POV: Carolyn is talking to Buddy and Christy. She's ON: smiling, animated, LAUGHING too loud at their jokes. Lester shakes his head. Ricky approaches him, wearing a waiter's uniform, carrying a tray of empty glasses.

RICKY   Excuse me. Don't you live on Robin Hood Trail? The house with the red door?

LESTER *(suspicious)* Yeah.

RICKY   I'm Ricky Fitts. I just moved into the house next to you.

LESTER   Oh. Hi, Ricky Fitts. I'm Lester Burnham.

RICKY   Hi, Lester Burnham.

          A beat. Lester looks away, scans the crowd, then
          downs the rest of his drink in one gulp. Ricky just
          stands there, watching him. Finally Lester turns
          back to Ricky: what does this kid want?

RICKY   Do you party?

LESTER   Excuse me?

RICKY   Do you get high?

          Lester's surprised, but instantly intrigued.

INT. HOTEL BALLROOM – MOMENTS LATER

          Carolyn and Buddy are deep in conversation.
          Christy has wandered off. Carolyn is nervous;
          Buddy seems amused.

CAROLYN   You know, I probably wouldn't even tell you this
          if I weren't a little tipsy, but... I am in complete
          awe of you. I mean, your firm is, hands down, the
          Rolls Royce of local Real Estate firms, and your
          personal sales record is, is, is very intimidating.
          You know, I'd love to sit down with you and
          just pick your brain, if you'd ever be willing.

I suppose, technically, I'm the 'competition,' but...
I mean, hey, I don't flatter myself that I'm even in
the same league as you...

BUDDY   I'd love to.

CAROLYN *(shocked)* Really?

BUDDY   Absolutely. Call my secretary and have her
schedule a lunch.

CAROLYN I'll do that. Thank you.

*They look at each other for a beat, then look
away. This situation is loaded and they both
know it.*

EXT. HOTEL – LATER

*Ricky and Lester stand next to a dumpster behind
the service entrance to the hotel, smoking a
JOINT.*

LESTER   ...did you ever see that movie, where the body's
walking around holding its own head? And then
the head goes down on that babe?

RICKY   *Re-Animator.*

47

Suddenly, the service entrance opens, and a large
CATERING BOSS in a cheap suit peers out at
them. Ricky hides the joint.

CATERING BOSS *(to Ricky)* Look. I'm not paying you to...
(eyes Lester, suspiciously)
...do whatever it is you're doing out here.

RICKY   Fine. So don't pay me.

CATERING BOSS Excuse me?

RICKY   I quit. So you don't have to pay me.
Now, leave me alone.

CATERING BOSS Asshole.

He goes back inside. Lester looks at Ricky,
who shrugs.

LESTER   I think you just became my personal hero.
(then)
Doesn't that make you nervous, just quitting your
job like that? Well, I guess when you're all of,
what? Sixteen?

RICKY   Eighteen. (then)
I just do these gigs as a cover. I have other
sources of income. But my dad interferes less in
my life when I pretend to be an upstanding young
citizen with a respectable job.

CAROLYN *(O.C.)* Lester?

> *Carolyn is standing in the open service entrance.*
> *Lester quickly hides the joint behind his back.*

CAROLYN What are you doing?

LESTER Honey, this is...
(laughs)
Ricky Fitts. This is Ricky Fitts.

RICKY I'm Ricky Fitts, I just moved in the house next to you. I go to school with your daughter.

LESTER With Jane? Really?

RICKY Yeah. Jane.

CAROLYN Hi.
(then, to Lester)
I'm ready to go. I'll meet you out front.

> *And she goes back inside.*

LESTER Uh-oh. I'm in trouble. Nice meeting you, Ricky Fitts. Thanks for the, uh, thing.

RICKY Any time.

> *Lester goes inside.*

RICKY *(calls after him)* Lester. If you want any more, you
know where I live.

INT. BURNHAM HOUSE – FAMILY ROOM – LATER

> *Jane and Angela are watching MTV.*
> *We HEAR the back door open.*

JANE   Oh, shit. They're home. Quick, let's go up to my
room.

> *Jane switches off the TV.*

ANGELA   I should say hi to your dad.
(off Jane's look)
I don't want to be rude.

> *She starts toward the kitchen. Jane doesn't*
> *like this.*

INT. BURNHAM HOUSE – KITCHEN – CONTINUOUS

> *Lester enters and opens the refrigerator.*

ANGELA *(O.C.)* Nice suit.

> *He turns, and is instantly transfixed by:*
> *His POV: Angela leans against the counter,*
> *twirling her hair.*

ANGELA You're looking good, Mr. Burnham.

She starts toward him.

ANGELA Last time I saw you, you looked kind of wound up.
(spots something)
Ooh, is that root beer?

*She reaches inside the refrigerator to grab a
bottle. As she does, she moves to place her other
hand casually on Lester's shoulder. He sees it
coming. Everything SLOWS DOWN, and all sound
FADES...*

*EXTREME CLOSE UP on her hand as it briefly
touches his shoulder in SLOW MOTION. We
HEAR only the amplified BRUSH of her fingers
against the fabric of his suit, and its unnatural,
hollow ECHO...*

*BACK IN REAL TIME: She grabs the root beer
and smiles at him. CLOSE on Lester: his eyes
narrow slightly, then: he cups her face in his
hands and kisses her. She seems shocked, but
doesn't resist as he pulls her toward him with
surprising strength. He breaks the kiss, looking at
her in awe, then he reaches up and touches his
lips. His eyes widen as he pulls a ROSE PETAL
from his mouth right before we SMASH CUT TO:*

INT. BURNHAM HOUSE – KITCHEN – CONTINUOUS

> *Angela is back against the counter, drinking the root beer. Lester stands by the refrigerator, gazing at her, still lost in fantasy.*

ANGELA   I love root beer, don't you?

> *Jane watches from the doorway to the family room, feeling incredibly awkward in her own home. Carolyn enters from the dining room. Lester snaps out of it and grabs a root beer from the refrigerator.*

JANE   Mom, you remember Angela.

CAROLYN *(her sales smile)* Yes, of course!

JANE   I forgot to tell you, she's spending the night. Is that okay?

LESTER   Sure!

> *He takes a sip of his root beer, but it goes down the wrong way and he starts COUGHING violently.*

INT. BURNHAM HOUSE – JANE'S BEDROOM
– LATER THAT NIGHT

> *Angela lays on the bed, in bra and panties,*
> *reading a magazine. Jane, in an oversized T shirt,*
> *plays a video game on her computer.*

JANE   I'm sorry about my dad.

ANGELA Don't be. I think it's funny.

JANE   Yeah, to you, he's just another guy who wants to
jump your bones. But to me... he's just too
embarrassing to live.

ANGELA Your mom's the one who's embarrassing.
What a phony.

> *Jane glances at Angela, irritated.*

ANGELA Your dad's actually kind of cute.

JANE   Shut up.

INT. BURNHAM HOUSE – HALLWAY – CONTINUOUS

> *Lester, still in his suit, stands outside Jane's room,*
> *his ear up against the door. He can't believe what*
> *he's hearing.*

ANGELA *(O.C.)* He is. If he just worked out a little,
he'd be hot.

**INT. BURNHAM HOUSE – JANE'S ROOM
– CONTINUOUS**

JANE   Shut up.

ANGELA   Oh, come on. Like you've never sneaked a peek
at him in his underwear? I bet he's got a big dick.

JANE   You are so grossing me out right now.

ANGELA   *(really enjoying this)* If he built up his chest and
arms, I would totally fuck him.

           *Jane covers her ears and starts SINGING to
           drown her out.*

INT. BURNHAM HOUSE – HALLWAY – CONTINUOUS

           *Lester, still listening, looks like he's about to
           implode.*

ANGELA   *(O.C.) (laughs)* I would! I would suck your dad's
big fat dick, and then I would fuck him 'til his
eyes rolled back in his head!
           (then)
What was that noise? Jane.

54

Jane's SINGING stops.

ANGELA *(O.C.)* I swear I heard something.

Panicked, Lester scurries down the hall.

**INT. BURNHAM HOUSE – JANE'S BEDROOM
– CONTINUOUS**

JANE   Yeah, it was the sound of you being a huge
         disgusting pig.

ANGELA   I'm serious.

         *We HEAR the sharp TAP of a penny being thrown
         against glass.*

ANGELA   See?

         Angela crosses to the window and looks out.

ANGELA   *(spots something)* Oh my God. Jane.

EXT. BURNHAM HOUSE – CONTINUOUS

         *We see Angela standing at the window in her
         underwear, looking down at us. Jane joins her and
         is immediately unnerved by:*

Their POV: In the Burnham's DRIVEWAY, the word 'JANE' is spelled out in FIRE.

INT. BURNHAM HOUSE – JANE'S BEDROOM – CONTINUOUS

ANGELA   It's that psycho next door. Jane, what if he worships you? What if he's got a shrine with pictures of you surrounded by dead people's heads and stuff?

JANE   Shit. I bet he's filming us right now.

ANGELA   *(intrigued)* Really?

EXT. BURNHAM HOUSE – CONTINUOUS

On VIDEO: We're across from Jane's window, looking in. Jane tries to shut the drapes, but Angela won't let her. Irritated, Jane retreats into the room. We ZOOM toward her, even as Angela poses in the window; we're clearly not interested in Angela. The ZOOM continues, searching for Jane, who has disappeared. Finally, we settle on the small make-up MIRROR where we see a REFLECTION of Jane, back at her computer. She's smiling. Then suddenly the DRAPES CLOSE and she's gone.

INT. FITTS HOUSE – RICKY'S BEDROOM
– CONTINUOUS

> *Ricky sits in darkness with his DIGICAM,*
> *videotaping. He lowers the camera and smiles...*
> *then something below catches his attention.*
> *He leans out the window to get a better look at:*

EXT. BURNHAM HOUSE – GARAGE – CONTINUOUS

> *Ricky's POV: Through a WINDOW on the side of*
> *the Burnham's GARAGE DOOR, we see Lester,*
> *still in his suit, digging through shelves against the*
> *back wall.*

INT. BURNHAM HOUSE – GARAGE – CONTINUOUS

> *Lester digs through stuff stored on the shelves,*
> *searching for something as if his very life*
> *depended on it.*

LESTER   Shit. Shit!

> *He yanks aside COLLEGE YEARBOOKS, a*
> *racquetball RACQUET, boxes of old HOT ROD*
> *MAGAZINES, an unopened remote-controlled*
> *MODEL JEEP KIT, stacks of old vinyl LPs... finally*
> *his face lights up when he finds: A pair of*
> *DUMBBELLS obviously unused for many years.*

Lester rips off his jacket and tie and unbuttons his shirt. He glances around, finding his REFLECTION in the WINDOW as he pulls off his shirt, then the T-shirt underneath. He eyes himself critically: Angela was right, he's not in bad shape. Just a few extra pounds around his middle that wouldn't be hard to shed. He kicks off his shoes and begins to step out of his pants.

INT. FITTS HOUSE – RICKY'S BEDROOM – CONTINUOUS

Ricky holds his Digicam up and starts to videotape.

EXT. BURNHAM HOUSE – GARAGE – CONTINUOUS

Ricky's POV, on VIDEO: Through a WINDOW on the side of the Burnham's garage, we see Lester step out of his pants and briefs. Then, naked except for his black socks, he grabs the dumbbells and starts lifting them, watching his reflection in the window as he does.

INT. FITTS HOUSE – RICKY'S BEDROOM
– CONTINUOUS

Ricky stands at the window, videotaping.

RICKY   Welcome to America's Weirdest Home Videos.

Suddenly we HEAR someone trying to open a locked door.

COLONEL *(O.C.)* Ricky!

Moving swiftly, Ricky pulls the drapes shut and switches on a light. His room is a haven of high-tech. A state-of-the-art multimedia COMPUTER crowds his desk, and high-end STEREO and VIDEO EQUIPMENT line the shelves, as well as HUNDREDS OF CDs. There is easily twenty thousand dollars worth of equipment in this room.

RICKY   Coming, Dad.

COLONEL (O.C.) You know I don't like locked doors in my house, boy.

Ricky opens the door. The Colonel stands outside, eyeing him.

RICKY   I'm sorry, I must have locked it by accident. So what's up?

> The Colonel holds out a small PLASTIC CUP
> WITH A CAP.

COLONEL I need a urine sample.

RICKY Wow. It's been six months already. Can I give it to
you in the morning? I just took a whiz.

COLONEL Yeah, I suppose.
> (an awkward beat)
Well. Good night, son.

> He disappears down the hall. Ricky smiles, shuts
> and locks his door. He puts the plastic cup on the
> shelf, then crosses to a MINI REFRIGERATOR in
> the corner of his room and takes out a cup-sized
> TUPPERWARE CONTAINER from the freezer,
> already filled with urine, albeit frozen, and places
> it on a saucer to thaw overnight.

INT. BURNHAM HOUSE – MASTER BEDROOM
– LATER THAT NIGHT

> Carolyn lies sleeping. Lester is awake, staring at
> the ceiling. After a moment, he gets up, taking
> care not to disturb Carolyn, and walks toward the
> bathroom.

INT. BURNHAM HOUSE – MASTER BATH
– CONTINUOUS

>*Lester enters and switches on the LIGHT. The room is filled with STEAM. Lester looks around, confused, then focuses on: His POV: Across from us, in a PEDESTAL BATHTUB, is Angela. She smiles and beckons us, and we MOVE CLOSER. ROSE PETALS float on the surface of the water, obscuring her naked body.*

ANGELA I've been waiting for you.

>*Lester kneels by the bathtub like a man in church.*

ANGELA You've been working out, haven't you? I can tell.

>*She arches her back and looks up at him provocatively.*

ANGELA I was hoping you'd give me a bath... I'm very, very dirty.

>*Lester gives her a hard look, then slowly slips his hand into the water between her legs. Her eyes widen and she throws her head back... and we SMASH CUT TO:*

INT. BURNHAM HOUSE – MASTER BEDROOM
– CONTINUOUS

> *CLOSE on Carolyn, her eyes wide, listening to the rhythmic BRUSH of Lester's hand as he masturbates under the covers. She flips over and faces him.*

CAROLYN What are you doing?

> *A beat.*

LESTER Nothing.

> *Carolyn switches on the bedside LIGHT.*

CAROLYN You were masturbating.

LESTER I was not.

CAROLYN Yes, you were.

> *He turns to her, trying to look innocent, then gives up.*

LESTER All right, so shoot me. I was whacking off.

> *Carolyn gets out of bed, repelled.*
> *Lester LAUGHS.*

LESTER   That's right. I was choking the bishop.
           Shaving the carrot. Saying hi to my monster.

CAROLYN That's disgusting.

LESTER   Well, excuse me, but I still have *blood* pumping
           through my veins!

CAROLYN So do I!

LESTER   Really? I'm the only one who seems to be doing
           anything about it.

CAROLYN Lester. I refuse to live like this. This is not a
           marriage.

LESTER   This hasn't been a marriage for years. But you
           were happy as long as I kept my mouth shut.
           Well, guess what? I've changed. And the new me
           whacks off when he feels horny, because you're
           obviously not going to help me out in that
           department.

CAROLYN Oh. I see. You think you're the only one who's
           sexually frustrated?

LESTER   I'm not? Well then, come on, baby! I'm ready.

CAROLYN *(furious)* Do not mess with me, mister, or I will
           divorce you so fast it'll make your head spin!

LESTER   On what grounds? I'm not a drunk, I don't fuck
         other women, I don't mistreat you, I've never hit
         you, or even tried to touch you since you made it
         so abundantly clear just how unnecessary you
         consider me to be. But. I did support you while
         you got your license. And some people might
         think that entitles me to half of what's yours.

         *She sinks into a chair, stunned. It's clear he
         knows where she's most vulnerable. He sees this,
         and likes it; it feels good to win for a change. He
         curls up under the covers contentedly.*

LESTER   Turn out the light when you come to bed, okay?

         CLOSE on Lester, smiling.

EXT. ROBIN HOOD TRAIL – EARLY MORNING

         *We're FLYING high above the neighborhood.
         Below us we see the two Jims, jogging. We
         APPROACH them steadily.*

LESTER   It's a great thing when you realize you still have
         the ability to surprise yourself. Makes you wonder
         what else you can do that you've forgotten about.

EXT. ROBIN HOOD TRAIL – CONTINUOUS

> *We're now at street level, FOLLOWING the two Jims.*

LESTER   Hey! You guys!

> *Still running, the Jims turn back in perfect unison, as Lester runs INTO FRAME, wearing a baggy sweatshirt and a pair of faded old sweatpants. The Jims slow down until he catches up, then the three men run together in the early morning light.*

JIM #2   Lester, I didn't know you ran.

LESTER   *(panting)* Well, I just started.

JIM #1   Good for you.

LESTER   I figured you guys might be able to give me some pointers. I need to shape up. Fast.

JIM #1   Well, are you just looking to lose weight, or do you want have increased strength and flexibility as well?

LESTER   I want to look good naked.

EXT. FITTS HOUSE - A SHORT TIME LATER

*The Colonel is washing his Ford Explorer,
squatting to scrub the bumper, when something
catches his eye: His POV: Lester and the Jims jog
down the street. The Colonel stands, scowling, as
Ricky comes out of the house, holding the URINE
SAMPLE in front of him.*

COLONEL What is this, the fucking gay pride parade?

*Lester breaks off from the two Jims and jogs up
to Ricky and the Colonel, out of breath. He grabs
hold of his knees and bends over, panting.*

LESTER Hey! Yo! Ricky!
(re: the Jims)
My entire life is passing before my eyes, and
those two have barely broken a sweat.

*He LAUGHS, and extends his hand to the
Colonel.*

LESTER Sorry, hi. Lester Burnham, I live next door.
We haven't met.

COLONEL *(shakes)* Colonel Frank Fitts, U.S. Marine Corps.

LESTER Whoa. Welcome to the neighborhood, sir.

He salutes the Colonel good-naturedly, grinning. The Colonel doesn't think it's funny. An awkward beat.

LESTER   So, Ricky, uh, I was thinking about the, uh... I was gonna... the movie we talked about...

RICKY   *(quickly)* Re-Animator.

LESTER   Yeah!

RICKY   You want to borrow it?
(before Lester can answer)
Okay, it's up in my room. Come on.

He heads into the house. Lester waves at the Colonel, then follows him. The Colonel watches them go, his eyes dark.

INT. FITTS HOUSE – RICKY'S BEDROOM – MOMENTS LATER

Ricky enters, followed by Lester.

RICKY   Can you hold this for a sec?

LESTER   Sure.

                    He gives the URINE SPECIMEN to Lester,
                    then locks the door.

RICKY   I don't think my dad would try to come in when
            somebody else is here, but you never know.

                    Ricky crosses to a bureau and opens a DRAWER.
                    He takes clothing out and piles it on his bed.

LESTER   *(re: urine sample)* What is this?

RICKY   Urine. I have to take a drug test every six months
            to make sure I'm clean.

LESTER   Are you kidding? You just smoked with me last
            night.

RICKY   It's not mine. One of my clients is a nurse in a
            pediatrician's office. I cut her a deal, she keeps
            me in clean piss.

                    Lester picks up a CD case from a shelf and
                    examines it.

LESTER   You like Pink Floyd?

RICKY   I like a lot of music.

LESTER   Man, I haven't listened to this album in years.

_____

He shakes his head, then puts the CD case down.
Ricky, having emptied the drawer, now removes a
FALSE BOTTOM, revealing rows of MARIJUANA,
tightly packed in ZIP-LOC BAGS.

RICKY   How much do you want?

LESTER   I don't know, it's been a while. How much is an
         ounce?

RICKY *(indicates bag)* Well, this is totally decent, and it's
         three hundred.

LESTER   Wow.

RICKY *(indicates another bag)* But this shit is top of the line.
         It's called G-13. Genetically engineered by the
         U.S. Government. Extremely potent. But a
         completely mellow high, no paranoia.

LESTER   Is that what we smoked last night?

RICKY   This is all I ever smoke.

LESTER   How much?

RICKY   Two grand.

LESTER   Jesus. Things have changed since 1973.

RICKY   You don't have to pay now. I know you're
         good for it.

         A beat.

LESTER   Thanks.

RICKY   *(hands him a bag)* There's a card in there with my
         beeper number, call me anytime day or night.
         And I only accept cash.

LESTER   *(looks around room)* Well, now I know how you can
         afford all this equipment. When I was your age, I
         flipped burgers all summer just to be able to buy
         an eight track.

RICKY   That sucks.

LESTER   No actually, it was great. All I did was party
         and get laid.
         (smiles)
         I had my whole life ahead of me...

RICKY   My dad thinks I pay for all this with catering jobs.
         (off Lester's look)
         Never underestimate the power of denial.

         Lester smiles. This kid's cool.

EXT. BURNHAM HOUSE – LATER

Carolyn, carrying a basket of fresh cut ROSES,
passes by the GARAGE WINDOW. From inside
the garage, we HEAR ROCK MUSIC. Carolyn
stops and SNIFFS the air, frowning. She peers
through the window.

Her POV: Lester, in a T-shirt and gym shorts, lies
on a new WEIGHT BENCH, doing bench presses
with shiny new BARBELLS.

INT. GARAGE – CONTINUOUS

ROCK MUSIC blasts from a new BOOMBOX on
the floor. The garage is in the process of
becoming Lester's sanctuary. An ugly but
comfortable 70s BOWL CHAIR has been pulled
out and cleaned off, his old hot rod magazines
strewn across it, and the remote-controlled
MODEL JEEP KIT is spread across a card table.
The SHELVES that Lester tore through earlier
have been dismantled, leaving a blank wall on
which now hangs a DART BOARD. Lester
finishes his last rep, straining, then puts the
weights in their rack and sits up. As he takes a
drag off a joint, the GARAGE DOOR suddenly
starts to open. Lester looks up, squinting at:

His POV: The door raises to reveal Carolyn,
silhouetted against the bright sunlight outside,
pointing a REMOTE at us.

LESTER   Uh-oh, mom's mad.

CAROLYN What the hell do you think you're doing?

LESTER   Bench presses. I'm going to wail on my pecs,
         and then I'm going to do my back.

CAROLYN I see you're smoking pot now. I'm so glad. I
         think using illegal psychotropic substances is a
         very positive example to set for our daughter.

LESTER   You're one to talk, you bloodless, money-
         grubbing freak.

CAROLYN *(hostile)* Lester. You have such hostility in you!

LESTER   Do you mind? I'm trying to work out here.
         (then, suggestively)
         Unless you want to spot me.

CAROLYN You will not get away with this. You can be sure
         of that!

         And she's gone. Lester leans back on the bench
         and grabs the weights.

LESTER   *(as he lifts)* That's. What. You. Think.

72

INT. BRAD'S OFFICE – DAY

> *Brad is seated behind his desk, reading a*
> *document. Lester sits across from him, smiling.*

BRAD *(reads)* '...my job consists of basically masking my
    contempt for the assholes in charge, and, at least
    once a day, retiring to the men's room so I can
    jerk off, while I fantasize about a life that doesn't
    so closely resemble hell.'
    (looks up at Lester)
    Well, you obviously have no interest in saving
    yourself.

LESTER *(laughs)* Brad, for fourteen years I've been a whore
    for the advertising industry. The only way I could
    save myself now is if I start firebombing.

BRAD Whatever. Management wants you gone by the
    end of the day.

LESTER Well, just what sort of severance package is
    'management' prepared to offer me? Considering
    the information I have about our editorial director
    buying pussy with company money.

> *A beat.*

LESTER Which I'm sure would interest the I.R.S., since it
    technically constitutes fraud. And I'm sure that
    some of our advertisers and rival publications

might like to know about it as well. Not to mention, Craig's wife.

Brad sighs.

BRAD   What do you want?

LESTER   One year's salary, with benefits.

BRAD   That's not going to happen.

LESTER   Well, what do you say I throw in a little sexual harassment charge to boot?

Brad LAUGHS.

BRAD   Against who?

LESTER   Against you.

Brad stops laughing.

LESTER   Can you prove you didn't offer to save my job if I'd let you blow me?

Brad leans back in his chair, studying Lester.

BRAD   Man. You are one twisted fuck.

LESTER   *(standing)* Nope. I'm just an ordinary guy with nothing to lose.

INT. OFFICE BUILDING – MOMENTS LATER

Exhilarated, Lester walks down a corridor, his belongings in a box on his shoulder. He's happier than he's been in years.

LESTER   Yeah!

INT. RESTAURANT – LATER THAT DAY

Carolyn sits at a table, lost in thought. There are two menus on the table. After a moment, Buddy Kane, the Real Estate King, joins her. Carolyn immediately becomes warm and gracious.

BUDDY   Carolyn.

CAROLYN   Buddy.

Carolyn smiles, genuinely touched that he remembers her name.

BUDDY   I'm so sorry I kept you waiting. Christy left for New York this morning, and... let's just say things were very hectic around the house.

CAROLYN   What's she doing in New York?

BUDDY   She's moving there.
         (off Carolyn's look)
         Yes. We are splitting up.

CAROLYN Buddy. I'm so sorry.

BUDDY   *(bitterly)* Yes, according to her, I'm too focused on
         my career. As if being driven to succeed is some
         sort of character flaw. Well, she certainly knew
         how to take advantage of the lifestyle my success
         afforded her. Oh. Wow.
         (then, laughing)
         Ah, it's for the best.

CAROLYN When I saw you two at the party the other night,
         you seemed perfectly happy.

BUDDY   Well, call me crazy, but it is my philosophy that in
         order to be successful, one must project an
         image of success, at all times.

         *He smiles, then opens his menu. Carolyn picks
         hers up mechanically, but continues to stare at
         him, enraptured, like a fervent Christian who's just
         come face to face with Jesus.*

EXT. HIGH SCHOOL CAMPUS – LATER THAT DAY

*Ricky stands with his DIGICAM, videotaping
something on the ground at his feet.
On VIDEO: A DEAD BIRD lays on the ground,
decomposing.*

ANGELA (O.C.) What are you doing?

*On VIDEO: The camera JERKS up to discover
Jane and Angela staring at us.*

RICKY (O.C.) I was filming this dead bird.

ANGELA Why?

RICKY (O.C.) Because it's beautiful.

*On VIDEO: Angela looks at Jane, trying not to
laugh.*

ANGELA I think maybe you forgot your medication today,
mental boy.

*On VIDEO: She falls out of frame as we ZOOM
toward Jane.*

RICKY (O.C.) Hi, Jane.

JANE *(uncomfortable)* Look. I want you to stop filming me.

Ricky lowers the Digicam.

RICKY   Okay.

*He looks at her, curious, his eyes searching hers.
She doesn't look away.*

ANGELA   Well, whatever.
       (to Jane)
       This is boring. Let's go.

JANE *(to Ricky)* Do you need a ride?

ANGELA *(to Jane)* Are you crazy? I don't want to end up
       hacked to pieces in a dumpster somewhere.

RICKY   It's okay. I'll walk. But thanks.

ANGELA   Yeah, see? He doesn't want to go anyway.
       C'mon, let's go.

*Angela starts off, but Jane doesn't follow. Ricky
smiles at her. She almost smiles back, then:*

JANE *(calls off to Angela)* I think I'm going to walk, too.

Angela stops and stares at her.

ANGELA   What? Jane, that's like, almost a *mile*.

EXT. TOP HAT MOTEL – LATER THAT DAY

>*Carolyn's Mercedes is parked next to a JAGUAR CONVERTIBLE with a VANITY LICENSE PLATE that reads 'R E KING.'*

INT. TOP HAT MOTEL – CONTINUOUS

>*Carolyn and Buddy are in the middle of sex.*

CAROLYN Yes! Oh, God! I love it!

BUDDY You like getting nailed by the king?

CAROLYN Oh yes! I love it! Fuck me, your majesty!

EXT. STREET – LATER THAT DAY

>*Lester's Toyota Camry cruises through the streets. We hear Lester SINGING along to 'AMERICAN WOMAN' on the STEREO.*

INT. TOYOTA CAMRY – CONTINUOUS

>*Lester is driving, smoking a joint.*

LESTER AMERICAN WOMAN, STAY AWAY FROM ME...
AMERICAN WOMAN, MAMA LET ME BE...

DON'T COME A HANGIN' AROUND MY DOOR...
I DON'T WANT TO SEE YOUR FACE NO MORE...

EXT. MR. SMILEY'S - CONTINUOUS

*Lester continues singing along to 'AMERICAN
WOMAN' as the Camry pulls into the parking lot
of a FAST FOOD RESTAURANT. Lester pulls up
to the drive-thru speaker box.*

DRIVE-THRU GIRL *(O.C.) (over speaker box)* Smile you're at
Mr. Smiley's.

Lester turns down the volume on the stereo.

LESTER   What?

DRIVE-THRU GIRL *(O.C.)* Would you like to try our new
bacon and egg fajita just a dollar twenty-nine for
a limited time only.

LESTER   Uh... no. But thank you.
(reading menu)
I'll have a Big Barn Burger, Smiley fries, and an
orange soda.

DRIVE-THRU GIRL *(O.C.)* Please drive up to the window,
thank you.

> *He pulls the car around to the WINDOW, where a teenage GIRL wearing a headset is waiting.*

DRIVE-THRU GIRL Smile, you're at Mr. Smiley's, that'll be four eighty-nine, please.

> *Lester pays her. As she hands him his food, he notices a SIGN in the corner of the window that reads: NOW TAKING APPLICATIONS*

COUNTER GIRL Would you like some Smiley Sauce?

LESTER No. No, actually... I'd like to fill out an application.

> *She stares at him, confused by his age and attire.*

COUNTER GIRL There's not jobs for manager, it's just for counter.

LESTER Good. I'm looking for the least possible amount of responsibility.

INT. MR. SMILEY'S – A SHORT TIME LATER

> *Lester sits at a booth with the MANAGER, a greasy kid wearing a white short sleeve shirt and a tie covered with the Mr. Smiley's logo. He looks over Lester's application, baffled.*

MANAGER I don't think you'd fit in here.

LESTER   I have fast food experience.

MANAGER   Yeah, like twenty years ago.

LESTER   Well, I'm sure there have been amazing
          technological advances in the industry, but surely
          you have some sort of training process. It seems
          unfair to presume I won't be able to learn.

          *The Manager sighs and runs a hand through his
          greasy hair, wondering what he could possibly
          have done to deserve this.*

INT. TOP HAT MOTEL – LATER THAT DAY

          Carolyn and Buddy are in bed, post-sex.

CAROLYN   That was exactly what I needed. The royal
          treatment, so to speak.

          They laugh.

CAROLYN   I was *so* stressed out.

BUDDY   Know what I do when I feel like that?

CAROLYN   What?

BUDDY   I fire a gun.

Carolyn sits up, eager to learn from the master.

CAROLYN *(intrigued)* Really.

BUDDY   Oh yeah, I go to this little firing range downtown, and I just pop off a few rounds.

CAROLYN *(embarrassed)* I've never fired a gun before.

BUDDY   Oh, you've gotta try it. Nothing makes you feel more powerful.
(smiles seductively)
Well, almost nothing.

Carolyn is quick to pick up her cue and kisses him, ready for another round.

EXT. SUBURBAN STREET – LATER THAT DAY

Ricky and Jane walk along without speaking. He seems comfortable with the silence; she doesn't. After a beat:

JANE So how do you like your new house?

RICKY   I like it.

A beat.

JANE The people who used to live there fed these stray cats, so they were always around, and it drove my mother nuts. And then she cut down their tree.

An automobile FUNERAL PROCESSION appears and begins to pass them slowly.

RICKY Have you ever known anybody who died?

JANE No. *(a beat)* Have you?

RICKY No, but I did see this homeless woman who froze to death once. Just laying there on the sidewalk. She looked really sad.

They watch the FUNERAL CARS pass.

RICKY I got that homeless woman on video.

JANE Why would you film that?

RICKY Because it was amazing.

JANE What was amazing about it?

A beat.

RICKY When you see something like that, it's like God is looking right at you, just for a second. And if you're careful, you can look right back.

JANE   And what do you see?

RICKY   Beauty.

INT. FITTS HOUSE – KITCHEN – MOMENTS LATER

> *Barbara Fitts sits at the kitchen table, staring off into space as if hypnotized. Behind her, Ricky enters, followed by Jane.*

RICKY   Mom, I want you to meet somebody.
(no response)
Mom.

> *Barbara's eyes flutter and she turns to him slowly.*

BARBARA *(pleasant)* Yes?

RICKY   I want you to meet somebody. This is Jane.

JANE   Hi.

BARBARA   Oh, my. I apologize for the way things look around here.

> *Jane glances around. The room is spotless.*

INT. FITTS HOUSE – THE COLONEL'S STUDY
– MOMENTS LATER

> *We HEAR KEYS TURNING in the lock, then the door opens and Ricky enters, holding a RING OF KEYS, followed by Jane.*

RICKY   This is where my dad hides out.

> *GLASS CASES filled with GUNS line the walls.*

JANE   I take it he's got a thing for guns.

> *Ricky crosses to a built-in CABINET behind the desk.*

RICKY   You got to see this one thing...

> *He unlocks the cabinet and opens it, revealing shelves stacked with WAR MEMORABILIA.*

RICKY   My dad would kill me if he knew I was in here.

JANE   Did you steal his keys?

RICKY   No. One of my clients is a locksmith. He was short on cash one night, so I let him pay me in trade.

*He reaches into the cabinet and carefully removes
an oval CHINA PLATTER, which he hands to
Jane. She examines it.*

RICKY   Turn it over.

*CLOSE on the bottom of the plate: A small
SWASTIKA is imprinted in the center.*

JANE   Oh my God.

RICKY   It's like official state china of the Third Reich.
There's a whole subculture of people who collect
this Nazi shit. But my dad just has this one thing.

*He puts the platter back into the cabinet and
shuts the door, then notices Jane looking at
him oddly.*

RICKY   What's wrong?

JANE   Nothing.

RICKY *(concerned)* No, you're scared of me.

JANE   No I'm not.

But she is. Ricky studies her.

RICKY   You want to see the most beautiful thing I've ever
filmed?

INT. FITTS HOUSE – RICKY'S BEDROOM
– MOMENTS LATER

> *On VIDEO: We're in an empty parking lot on a cold, gray day. Something is floating across from us... it's an empty, wrinkled, white PLASTIC BAG. We follow it as the wind carries it in a circle around us, sometimes whipping it about violently, or, without warning, sending it soaring skyward, then letting it float gracefully down to the ground... Jane and Ricky sit on the bed, watching his WIDE-SCREEN TV.*

RICKY   It was one of those days when it's a minute away from snowing. And there's this electricity in the air, you can almost hear it, right? And this bag was just... dancing with me. Like a little kid begging me to play with it. For fifteen minutes. That's the day I realized that there was this entire life behind things, and this incredibly benevolent force that wanted me to know there was no reason to be afraid. Ever.

> *A beat.*

RICKY   Video's a poor excuse, I know. But it helps me remember... I need to remember...

> *Now Jane is watching him.*

RICKY *(distant)* Sometimes there's so much beauty in the
world I feel like I can't take it... and my heart is
going to cave in.

After a moment, Jane takes his hand. Then she
leans in and kisses him softly on the lips. His eyes
scan hers, curious to see how she reacts to this...

JANE *(suddenly)* Oh my God. What time is it?

INT. BURNHAM HOUSE – DINING ROOM
– MOMENTS LATER

Lester sits at the table in sloppy clothes, eating
his dinner voraciously and drinking beer from a
bottle. Across from him, Carolyn picks at her
food, watching him with contempt. EASY-
LISTENING MUSIC plays on the STEREO.

We HEAR the back door SLAM, then Jane enters
and quickly takes her seat at the table.

JANE Sorry I'm late.

CAROLYN *(overly cheerful)* No, no, that's quite all right,
dear. Your father and I were just discussing his
day at work.
(to Lester)
Why don't you tell our daughter about it, honey?

Jane stares at both her parents, apprehensive.
Lester looks at Carolyn darkly, then flashes a
'you-asked-for-it' grin.

LESTER   Janie, today I quit my job. And then I told my
         boss to fuck himself, and then I blackmailed him
         for almost sixty thousand dollars. Pass the
         asparagus.

CAROLYN Your father seems to think this kind of behavior
         is something to be proud of.

LESTER   And your mother seems to prefer I go through life
         like a fucking prisoner while she keeps my dick in
         a mason jar under the sink.

CAROLYN *(ashen)* How dare you speak to me that way in
         front of her? And I marvel that you can be so
         contemptuous of me, on the same day that you
         lose your job!

LESTER   Lose it? I didn't lose it. It's not like, 'Oops,
         where'd my job go?' I *quit*. Someone pass me the
         asparagus.

CAROLYN Oh! Oh! And I want to thank you for putting me
         under the added pressure of being the sole
         breadwinner now—

LESTER   I already have a job.

CAROLYN *(not stopping)* No, no, don't give a second
thought as to who's going to pay the mortgage.
We'll just leave it all up to Carolyn. You mean,
you're going to take care of *everything* now,
Carolyn? Yes. I don't mind. I really don't. You
mean, *everything*? You don't mind having the sole
responsibility, your husband feels he can just quit
his job—

LESTER *(overlapping)* Will someone pass me the fucking
asparagus?

JANE *(rises)* Okay, I'm not going to be a part of this—

LESTER *(means it)* Sit down.

> *Jane does so, surprised and intimidated by the
> power in his voice. Lester gets up, crosses to the
> other side of the table to get a PLATE OF
> ASPARAGUS, then sits again as he serves
> himself.*

LESTER I'm sick and tired of being treated like I don't
exist. You two do whatever you want to do
whenever you want to do it and I don't complain.
All I want is the same courtesy—

CAROLYN *(overlapping)* Oh, you don't complain? Oh,
excuse me. Excuse me. I must be psychotic then,
if you don't complain. What is this?! Am I locked
away in a padded cell somewhere, hallucinating?

That's the only explanation I can think of—
Lester hurls the plate of asparagus against the wall with such force it SHATTERS, frightening Carolyn and Jane.

LESTER *(casual)* Don't interrupt me, honey.

He goes back to eating his meal, as if nothing unusual has happened. Carolyn sits in her chair, shivering with rage. Jane just stares at the plate in front of her.

LESTER Oh, and another thing. From now on, we're going to alternate our dinner music. Because frankly, and I don't think I'm alone here, I'm really tired of this Lawrence Welk shit.

INT. BURNHAM HOUSE – JANE'S BEDROOM – THAT NIGHT

Jane is sitting on her bed. There is a KNOCK at the door.

JANE Go. Away.

CAROLYN (O.C.) Honey, please let me in.

Jane rolls her eyes, crosses to the door and lets Carolyn in.

CAROLYN I wish that you hadn't witnessed that awful
scene tonight. But in a way, I'm glad.

JANE Why, so I could see what freaks you and Dad
really are?

CAROLYN Me?

She stares at Jane, then starts to cry.

JANE Aw, Christ, Mom.

CAROLYN *(tearful)* No, I'm glad because you're old enough
now to learn the most important lesson in life:
you cannot count on anyone except yourself.
(sighs)
You cannot count on anyone except yourself.
It's sad, but true, and the sooner you learn it,
the better.

JANE Look, Mom, I really don't feel like having a Kodak
moment here, okay?

Carolyn suddenly SLAPS Jane, hard.

CAROLYN You ungrateful little brat. Just look at everything
you have. When I was your age, I lived in a
duplex. We didn't even have our own house.

Embarrassed, she quickly leaves. Jane looks in a
mirror and rubs her cheek, then crosses to the
window and looks out.

EXT. FITTS HOUSE – CONTINUOUS

Jane's POV: We're across from Ricky's room,
looking in. He stands at the window with his
DIGICAM, videotaping us. On the WIDE-SCREEN
TV behind him, we see Jane standing in her
window as she looks across at him. She waves.
Ricky just keeps videotaping. A beat, then she
starts to take off her shirt.

INT. FITTS HOUSE – RICKY'S BEDROOM
– CONTINUOUS

We're behind Ricky as he videotapes Jane in her
window. She has now removed her shirt. She
stands there in her bra, then reaches behind her
back to unhook the bra.

On VIDEO: We ZOOM toward her as she takes off
her bra clumsily. She's obviously embarrassed,
but she's gone this far and there's no turning
back. She stands there with her breasts exposed,
trying to look defiant, but she's achingly
vulnerable...

> Suddenly, the door is thrown open and the
> Colonel enters, incensed. Startled, Ricky turns
> around. As soon as his eyes meet his father's, he
> knows what's up.

COLONEL You little bastard—

> Ricky scrambles to dodge his father, but the
> Colonel is too fast; he punches Ricky in the face,
> knocking him to the floor.

COLONEL How did you get in there?

EXT. BURNHAM HOUSE – CONTINUOUS

> From her window, Jane watches, pulling the
> drapes in front of her.

EXT. FITTS HOUSE – CONTINUOUS

> Jane's POV: In the WINDOW across from us, the
> Colonel proceeds to give Ricky a serious beating,
> punching his face.

INT. FITTS HOUSE – RICKY'S BEDROOM
– CONTINUOUS

> *Ricky's lip is bleeding, but he maintains a steady gaze at his father during this violence.*

COLONEL *(unnerved)* How!? How?! C'mon, get up! Fight back, you little pussy!

RICKY No, sir. I won't fight you.

> *The Colonel grabs him by the collar.*

COLONEL How did you get in there?

RICKY I picked the lock, sir.

COLONEL What were you looking for? Money? Are you on dope again?

RICKY No, sir. I wanted to show my girlfriend your Nazi plate.

> *A beat.*

COLONEL Girlfriend?

RICKY Yes, sir. She lives next door.

> *The Colonel glances toward the window.*

>His POV: In the WINDOW across from us, Jane
>peeks out from behind the drape. She quickly
>pulls it shut.

RICKY   Her name's Jane.

>A beat. The Colonel is suddenly, deeply shamed.

COLONEL This is for your own good, boy. You have no
         respect for other people's things, for authority,
         for...

RICKY   Sir, I'm sorry.

COLONEL You can't just go around doing whatever you
         feel like, you can't—there are rules in life—

RICKY   Yes, sir.

COLONEL You need structure, you need discipline—

RICKY   *(simultaneous)* Discipline. Yes, sir, thank you for
         trying to teach me. Don't give up on me, Dad.

>The Colonel stands, still breathing heavily.
>Tenderness fills his face, and he reaches out to
>touch Ricky's cheek.

COLONEL Oh, Ricky...

>But something keeps him from doing it.

COLONEL You stay out of there.

> He leaves. Ricky gets up and goes to his bureau.
> He looks at his reflection in the mirror, calmly
> takes a cloth and starts to wipe the blood from
> his face.

> FADE TO BLACK.
> In darkness, we HEAR repetitive GUNSHOTS.
> FADE IN:

INT. INDOOR FIRING RANGE – ONE MONTH LATER

> Carolyn, wearing PROTECTIVE HEADGEAR, is
> holding a GLOCK 19 AUTOMATIC REVOLVER
> with both hands, FIRING it directly at us.
> She empties a round and stands there,
> exhilarated. An ATTENDANT approaches with a
> new round of ammunition.

ATTENDANT *(loading gun)* I gotta say, Mrs. Burnham, when
you first came here I thought you would be
hopeless. But you're a natural.

CAROLYN Well, all I know is... I love shooting this gun!

> And she starts FIRING again.

INT. MERCEDES-BENZ ML320 – LATER

Bobby Darin sings 'DON'T RAIN ON MY PARADE' on the RADIO. Carolyn SINGS along as she drives. Her face has lost its usual resolute determination; she's actually enjoying herself spontaneously, and the lack of her usual self-consciousness allows us to see just how beautiful she is. ANGLE ON the GLOCK 19 sitting on the passenger seat amidst some CDs. Carolyn takes the gun and holds it at arm's length, admiring it as she continues to SING.

EXT. ROBIN HOOD TRAIL – CONTINUOUS

The Mercedes turns onto Robin Hood Trail.

INT. MERCEDES-BENZ ML320 – CONTINUOUS

Carolyn's POV: We turn into the Burnham driveway. A 1970 PONTIAC FIREBIRD with racing stripes blocks our access to the garage. CLOSE on Carolyn: She doesn't like having things in her way.

INT. BURNHAM HOUSE – FAMILY ROOM
– MOMENTS LATER

> *Lester's REMOTE-CONTROLLED MODEL JEEP is zooming across the floor of the family room, expertly manoeuvring corners and narrowly avoiding crashing. Lester is sprawled on the couch in his underwear, drinking a BEER and controlling the car. His working out is beginning to produce results. The room, too, seems changed: sloppier, more lived in. Carolyn enters through the kitchen, flushed and angry. She just stands there, staring at Lester. After a moment, he looks up at her.*

LESTER   What?

CAROLYN   Ah, whose car is that out front?

LESTER   Mine. 1970 Pontiac Firebird. The car I always wanted and now I have it. I rule!

CAROLYN   Where's the Camry?

LESTER   I traded it in.

CAROLYN   Shouldn't you have consulted me first?

LESTER   Hmm, let me think... No. You never drove it. *(then)* Have you done something different? You look great.

CAROLYN *(brusque)* Where's Jane?

LESTER   Jane not home. We have the whole house to
ourselves.

> *He smiles at her playfully. She stares back,*
> *annoyed. It's the same look she had at the*
> *beginning, when he dropped his briefcase, but*
> *whatever power that look had is gone. Lester just*
> *LAUGHS.*

LESTER Christ, Carolyn. When did you become so... joyless?

CAROLYN *(taken aback)* Joyless?! I am not joyless! There
happens to be a lot about me that you don't
know, mister smarty man. There is plenty of joy in
my life.

LESTER *(leaning toward her)* Whatever happened to that
girl who used to fake seizures at frat parties when
she got bored? And who used to run up to the
roof of our first apartment building to flash the
traffic helicopters? Have you totally forgotten
about her? Because I haven't.

> *His face is close to hers, and suddenly the*
> *atmosphere is charged. She pulls back*
> *automatically, but it's clear she's drawn to him.*
> *He smiles, and moves even closer, holding his*
> *beer loosely balanced. Then, just before their*
> *lips meet...*

CAROLYN *(barely audible)* Lester. You're going to spill beer
on the couch.

> *She's immediately sorry she said it, but it's too*
> *late. His smile fades, and the moment is gone.*

LESTER   So what? It's just a couch.

CAROLYN This is a four thousand dollar sofa upholstered in
Italian silk. This is not 'just a couch'.

LESTER   It's just a couch!

> *He stands and gestures toward all the things in*
> *the room.*

LESTER   This isn't *life*. This is just *stuff*. And it's become
more important to you than living. Well, honey,
that's just nuts.

> *Carolyn stares at him, on the verge of tears,*
> *then turns and walks out of the room before*
> *he can see her cry.*

LESTER *(calls after her)* I'm only trying to help you.

INT. FITTS HOUSE – RICKY'S BEDROOM – NIGHT

> *On VIDEO: Jane lays in Ricky's bed, wearing a*
> *tank top. She glances at us.*

JANE *(shy)* Don't.

> *We're watching the WIDE-SCREEN TV in
> Ricky's room. A CORD leads from the TV to
> Ricky's DIGICAM. Ricky holds the camera,
> sitting naked in a chair. It's been almost a month
> since his father beat him up, and there are still
> slight SCARS on his face. He's aiming his
> camera at Jane.*

RICKY Why?

JANE *(re: image on TV)* It's weird, watching myself. I don't
like how I look.

RICKY I can't believe you don't know how beautiful you
are.

JANE I'm not going to sit here for that shit.

> *She gets out of bed, takes his Digicam and
> focuses it on him. We see his image on the TV
> as she videotapes.*

JANE Ha. How does it feel now?

RICKY Fine.

JANE You don't feel naked?

RICKY I am naked.

JANE   You know what I mean.

              Jane ZOOMS in on his face, which remains
              placid.

JANE   Tell me about being in the hospital.

              Ricky smiles.

RICKY   When I was fifteen, my dad caught me smoking
              dope. He totally freaked and decided to send me
              to military school. I told you his whole thing about
              structure and discipline, right?
              (laughs)
              Well, of course, I got kicked out. Dad and I had
              this huge fight, and he hit me... and then the
              next day at school, some kid made a crack
              about my haircut, and... I just snapped. I wanted
              to kill him. And I would have. Killed him. If they
              hadn't pulled me off.
              (then)
              That's when my dad put me in the hospital.
              Then they drugged me up and left me in there
              for two years.

JANE   Wow. You must really hate him.

RICKY   He's not a bad man.

              He grabs a half-smoked JOINT from an ashtray
              and lights it.

JANE   Well... you better believe I'd hate my father if he
        did something like that to me.
        (laughs)
        Wait. I do hate my father.

RICKY   Why?

        *He passes her the joint, then takes the Digicam
        and focuses it on her. We see her image on the
        TV as he videotapes.*

JANE   He's a total asshole and he's got this crush on my
        friend Angela and it's disgusting.

RICKY   You'd rather he had the crush on you?

JANE   Gross, no! But it'd be nice if I was anywhere near
        as important to him as she is.
        (then)
        I know you think my dad's harmless, but you're
        wrong. He's doing massive psychological
        damage to me.

RICKY   How?

        *Jane looks into the camera, a loopy, stoned grin
        on her face.*

JANE   Well, now, I too need structure. A little fucking
        discipline.

They LAUGH. She lays back on the bed.

JANE   I'm serious, though. How could he not be
        damaging me? I need a father who's a role
        model, not some horny geek-boy who's gonna
        spray his shorts whenever I bring a girlfriend
        home from school.
        (snorts)
        What a lame-o. Somebody really should put him
        out of his misery.

        Her mind wanders for a beat.

RICKY   Want me to kill him for you?

        Jane looks at him and sits up.

JANE   Yeah, would you?

RICKY   *(smiles)* It'll cost you.

JANE   Well, I've been baby-sitting since I was about
        ten. I've got almost three thousand dollars.
        'Course, I was saving it up for a boob job.

        *She stands and sticks out her breasts, then falls
        back on the bed, LAUGHING.*

JANE   But my tits can wait, huh?

RICKY   You know, that's not a very nice thing to do,
          hiring somebody to kill your dad.

JANE   Well, I guess I'm just not a very nice girl, then, am I?

          She smiles dreamily at him. He turns the Digicam
          off and the TV screen goes BLUE. He lowers the
          camera and looks at her intently.

JANE   *(suddenly nervous)* You know I'm not serious, right?

RICKY   Of course.

          He puts the Digicam down and joins Jane
          on the bed. A long moment where neither of
          them speaks. He caresses her hair, gazing
          into her eyes.

RICKY   Do you know how lucky we are to have found
          each other?

          FADE TO BLACK.

          FADE IN:

EXT. ROBIN HOOD TRAIL – EARLY MORNING

          We're FLYING above Robin Hood Trail. We see
          the BURNHAM'S HOUSE below us as we
          APPROACH it steadily.

LESTER   Remember those posters that said, 'Today is the
          first day of the rest of your life?' Well, that's true
          of every day except one.
          (a beat)
          The day you die.

>   *We're almost on top of the Burnham house
>   now, as Lester, wearing sweatpants and running
>   shoes, bursts out of the front door and dashes
>   up the driveway.*

EXT. ROBIN HOOD TRAIL – A SHORT TIME LATER

>   *We're now at street level, as Lester runs toward
>   us. He carries a WALKMAN and wears
>   EARPHONES, and we HEAR ROCK MUSIC as he
>   runs. The endorphins have kicked in, and Lester
>   grins, reveling in the sheer physical pleasure of
>   his body.*

INT. BURNHAM HOUSE – KITCHEN
– A SHORT TIME LATER

>   *The blender GRINDS as Lester, still in his
>   sweatpants, makes himself a high-protein shake.
>   He's in excellent shape; even his posture has
>   changed, and he moves with the confident, easy
>   swagger of an athlete. Jane watches him blankly
>   from the kitchen table. Carolyn enters. Lester*

*leans against the counter, drinking his shake
directly from the blender pitcher, eyeing her. He's
got a newfound sexual energy that makes her
uncomfortable, and he knows it. Carolyn quickly
rinses off her coffee cup, avoiding his eyes, and
starts out.*

CAROLYN Jane, hurry up. I've got a very important
appointment—

JANE   Mom, is it okay if Angela sleeps over tonight?

*Jane looks at Lester to see how he reacts.
He doesn't.*

CAROLYN Well, of course, she's always welcome.
(on her way out)
You know, I thought maybe you two had a fight.
I haven't seen her around here in a while.

*And she's gone. Jane continues staring at her
father. Finally, he glances over at her.*

LESTER   What?

JANE *(nervous)* I've been too embarrassed to bring her
over. Because of you, and the way that you
behave.

LESTER   What are you talking about? I've barely even
spoken to her.

JANE *(angry)* Dad! You stare at her all the time, like you're drunk! It's disgusting!

LESTER *(angry himself)* You better watch yourself, Janie, or you're going to turn into a real bitch, just like your mother.
Jane is stunned. She quickly rises, trying to get out of the kitchen before she starts crying.
ANGLE on Lester, and the immediate regret in his eyes.

LESTER *(under his breath)* Fuck.

INT. FITTS HOUSE – UPSTAIRS HALLWAY – CONTINUOUS

We're outside Ricky's room, MOVING slowly toward the open door, through which we can see Ricky, standing at his bureau mirror, combing his hair. The scars on his face are almost gone now.

A REVERSE ANGLE reveals the Colonel standing outside the door looking in, watching Ricky with great tenderness. Then Ricky looks up at him, and the Colonel is suddenly self-conscious.

COLONEL *(brusque)* You ready to go?

RICKY Oh, I don't need a ride. I'm going to go in with Jane and her mom.

EXT. FITTS HOUSE – FRONT PORCH
– MOMENTS LATER

Ricky emerges from the house, followed by the Colonel, who watches his son as he heads toward the Burnham house.

His POV: Carolyn waves from the Mercedes, flashing an insincere smile. Jane leans forward from the passenger seat and glares at us. As Ricky starts to get in the car, Lester emerges from the house in his sweatpants.

LESTER   Yo, Ricky. How's it going?

RICKY   Pretty decent, Mr. Burnham.

Ricky pulls his door shut, but not before Lester mouths 'call me' and Ricky gives a slight nod in acknowledgment. CLOSE on the Colonel's face: he looks confused. As the Mercedes backs out of the driveway, Lester glances over at him.

Lester's POV: The Colonel watches the car driving off, then looks at us. His face tightens. Lester studies him for a moment, then grins and salutes before going inside the house. CLOSE on the Colonel, deeply troubled.

INT. FITTS HOUSE – RICKY'S ROOM
– MOMENTS LATER

The door swings open silently and the Colonel enters. He starts going through Ricky's bureau. He opens the DRAWER in which we know Ricky keeps his marijuana, but he doesn't discover its false bottom. He stands and looks around, his eyes finally landing on: the DIGICAM and a stack of CASSETTES on a shelf. The camera is still connected to the TV. The Colonel turns on the TV, examines the Digicam and presses 'play.' The TV's blank screen suddenly gives way to...

On VIDEO: Barbara Fitts sits at the kitchen table, staring off into space. The Colonel watches, at first baffled, then impatient. He takes the cassette out of the Digicam and inserts another. On the TV screen we see...

On VIDEO: Through the Burnham's GARAGE WINDOW, we see Lester step out of his pants and briefs. Then, naked except for his black socks, he grabs the dumbbells and starts lifting them, watching his reflection in the window as he does... The Colonel sinks slowly onto Ricky's bed, mesmerized.

INT. MR. SMILEY'S – LATER

> *Lester, wearing a Mr. Smiley's uniform, is happily flipping burgers on a grill.*

CO-WORKER Hey Lester, I need that Super Smiley with cheese, A.S.A.P.

LESTER You need more than that, my little hombre.

> *Lester looks up suddenly when he HEARS:*

CAROLYN *(O.C.) (over speakers)* What's good here?

BUDDY *(O.C.) (over speakers)* Nothing.

CAROLYN *(O.C.) (over speakers)* Then I guess we'll just have to be bad, won't we?
> *(then)*
> I think I'll have a double Smiley Sandwich and curly fries, and a vanilla shake.

BUDDY *(O.C.) (over speakers)* Make that two.

COUNTER GIRL *(O.C.) (over speakers)* Please drive around thank you.

> *Lester's face darkens, then... he smiles.*
> *He puts his spatula down.*

EXT. MR. SMILEY'S – CONTINUOUS

> *The Mercedes pulls around to the DRIVE-THRU*
> *WINDOW. Carolyn drives; Buddy sits beside her.*

CAROLYN I think we deserve a little junk food, after the
workout we had this morning.

BUDDY *(nuzzles her neck)* I'm flattered.

> *They are too involved with each other to notice*
> *Lester watching them from the drive-thru window.*

LESTER *(overly cheerful)* Smile! You're at Mr. Smiley's!

> *Carolyn almost jumps out of her skin.*

> *Lester leans out of the drive-thru window,*
> *grinning at her, holding bags filled with fast food.*
> *The Counter Girl stands next to him, staring*
> *blankly.*

LESTER Would you like to try our new beef and cheese
pot pie on a stick, just a dollar ninety-nine for a
limited time only?

> *Carolyn struggles to appear nonchalant.*

CAROLYN *(re: Buddy)* We were just at a seminar.
(then, all business)
Buddy, this is my—

LESTER   Her *husband*. We've met before, but something
          tells me you're going to remember me this time.

COUNTER GIRL   *(to Carolyn)* Whoa. You are so busted.

CAROLYN   *(flustered)* You know, this really doesn't concern
           you.

LESTER   Actually, Janeane is senior drive-thru manager, so
          you kind of are on her turf.
          (to Carolyn, quietly)
          So. This makes sense.

CAROLYN   *(miserable)* Oh, Lester—

LESTER   Honey, it's okay. I want you to be happy.
          (then)
          Would you like Smiley Sauce with that?

CAROLYN Lester, just stop it!

LESTER   Uh-uh. You don't get to tell me what to do.
          Ever again.

          Carolyn closes her eyes, defeated, then grabs the
          wheel, shifts gears and drives off.

EXT. TOP HAT MOTEL – A SHORT TIME LATER

> The sky is filled with ominous gray clouds. Wind whips garbage across the parking lot as Carolyn's Mercedes pulls in next to Buddy's Jaguar.

INT. MERCEDES-BENZ ML320 – CONTINUOUS

> Carolyn grips the wheel tightly, staring straight ahead. Buddy looks at her unhappily.

BUDDY   I'm sorry. I guess we should cool it for a while. I'm facing a potentially very expensive divorce.

CAROLYN Oh, no. I understand completely.
(sarcastic)
In order to be successful, one must project an image of success. At all times.

> She regrets it the second it's out of her mouth, and turns to him. He just looks at her sadly, then gets out of the car and shuts the door. She starts to CRY. As before, she SLAPS herself, hard.

CAROLYN Stop it. Stop it!

> She closes her eyes tight, trying to stop the tears, then suddenly SCREAMS as loud as she can.

EXT. TOP HAT MOTEL – CONTINUOUS

> Buddy's Jaguar speeds off, leaving the Mercedes
> alone in the parking lot. We can still HEAR
> Carolyn's muffled SCREAMING. There is a sound
> of distant THUNDER.

INT. BURNHAM HOUSE – GARAGE – THAT NIGHT

> It's RAINING outside. We HEAR ROCK MUSIC
> as Lester pumps iron. He puts the weights down
> and looks at his REFLECTION in the window:
> His POV: His arms are pumped. He smiles.
> He reaches under the bench and grabs a CIGAR
> BOX. Opening it, he digs through MARIJUANA
> PARAPHERNALIA, only to pull out an empty
> ZIP-LOC BAG.

LESTER   Shit.

INT. FITTS HOUSE – KITCHEN – MOMENTS LATER

> Ricky and the Colonel sit at the table, eating in
> silence. Barbara rinses off a pan at the sink, then
> stares at it as if she can't quite remember what
> she meant to do with it. We suddenly HEAR a
> BEEPING noise. Ricky pulls his BEEPER off his
> belt and checks it.

RICKY *(getting up)* I have to run next door. Jane left her
geometry book in my bag and she needs it to do
her homework.

*He heads into the hall. The Colonel watches him
go, uneasy.*

INT. ANGELA'S BMW – CONTINUOUS

*Angela drives, squinting through the windshield
as the wipers move back and forth.*

ANGELA So you and psycho boy are fucking on like, a
regular basis now, right?

JANE *(irritable)* No.

ANGELA Oh, come on. You can tell me. Does he have a
big dick?

JANE Look, I'm not gonna talk about his dick with you,
okay? It's not like that.

ANGELA Not like what? Doesn't he have one?
(then)
Why don't you want to talk about it? I mean,
I tell you every single detail about every guy
that I fuck.

JANE   Yeah, and maybe you shouldn't, all right? Maybe
              I don't really want to hear all that.

ANGELA Oh, so now that you have a boyfriend, you're like,
              above it?
              (rolls her eyes)
              We gotta get you a real man.

INT. FITTS HOUSE – KITCHEN – CONTINUOUS

*The Colonel rinses off his plate at the sink.
Something outside catches his eye, and he
cranes his neck to get a better look at...*

*His POV: Through the window over the sink, we
can see into the Burnham's GARAGE WINDOW.
Our view is blurred by the RAIN, but we see
Lester, his upper body pumped and glistening in
sweat as he counts out a wad of BILLS... and
then Ricky walks into view. The Colonel's face
tightens.*

*His POV: Lester drapes his arm around Ricky as
he gives him the money. We can only see Lester
from the waist up, so he looks naked.*

INT. BURNHAM HOUSE – GARAGE – CONTINUOUS

>   *Ricky, his hair wet from the rain, puts the cash in his pocket. Lester's arm remains draped around his shoulder.*

RICKY   *(grins)* You got any papers?

LESTER   Yeah, in the cigar box, right over there.
         (laughs)
         You know, put up a fight, dude! You are such a pushover. 'No I can't. Really. Okay.'

>   *And he slaps Ricky playfully on the chest. Ricky grins, then squats down and reaches under the weight bench.*

RICKY   You should learn to roll a joint.

>   *Lester sits in the bowl chair and leans back, his hands behind his head, watching Ricky roll the joint.*

INT. FITTS HOUSE – KITCHEN – CONTINUOUS

>   *The Colonel's POV: Lester leans back in his chair. We see only Ricky's back and shoulders as he rolls the joint. After a beat, Lester's jaw drops, then he throws his head back. From our perspective, it looks very much like Ricky is giving*

Lester a blow job. The Colonel watches,
incredulous. Then we HEAR a CAR
APPROACHING, and the Colonel glances over at:

His POV: Angela's BMW pulls into the driveway,
stopping behind Lester's Firebird. As Angela and
Jane get out and run toward the house, our
focus MOVES back to the GARAGE WINDOW.
Ricky stands, looking a little panicked. Lester
pulls on his T-shirt, and both he and Ricky cross
out of view.

INT. BURNHAM HOUSE – KITCHEN
– MOMENTS LATER

Lester leans nonchalantly against the counter.
Jane and Angela enter. Jane frowns when she
sees him.

LESTER   Oh. Hi.

JANE   Where's Mom?

LESTER   Don't know.

ANGELA   Hi, Mr. Burnham.

LESTER   Hi.

He's trying to remain cool, and doing a pretty good job.

ANGELA   Wow. Look at you. Have you been working out?

LESTER   Some.

Jane rolls her eyes and exits. Angela walks over to Lester.

ANGELA   You can really tell. Look at those arms.

She places her hand on his arm flirtatiously, looks up at him and smiles, fully expecting to intimidate him by doing so. But something has changed, and he isn't intimidated at all. He looks directly back at her, leans in and smiles slowly.

LESTER   You like muscles?

His voice is low and intense. She moves away, suddenly insecure.

ANGELA   I—I should probably go see what Jane's up to.

And she heads out quickly. Lester watches her go, baffled.

INT. FITTS HOUSE – RICKY'S ROOM – CONTINUOUS

> *Ricky enters, wet from the pouring rain, and crosses to his bureau, pulling the wad of CASH out of his pocket as he goes.*

COLONEL *(O.C.)* Where'd you get that?

> *Ricky turns, startled.*

> *His POV: The Colonel steps out of the shadows.*

> *Ricky takes a step back.*

RICKY   From my job.

COLONEL Don't lie to me.
> *(beat)*
> I saw you with him.

RICKY *(incredulous)* You were watching me?

COLONEL What did he make you do?

RICKY *(laughs)* Dad, you don't really think... me and
> Mr. Burnham?

COLONEL *(furious)* Don't you laugh at me!
> *(then)*
> I will not sit back and watch my only son become
> a cocksucker!

RICKY   Jesus, what is with you—

          *The Colonel BACKHANDS Ricky so hard it sends
          the boy sprawling.*

COLONEL I swear to God, I will throw you out of this house
          and never look at you again.

RICKY *(taken aback)* You mean that?

COLONEL Damn straight I do. I'd rather you were dead
          than be a fucking faggot.

          A beat. Ricky suddenly smiles. He gets up.

RICKY   You're right. I suck dick for money.

COLONEL Boy—

RICKY   Two thousand dollars. I'm that good.

COLONEL Get out.

RICKY   And you should see me fuck. I'm the best piece
          of ass in three states.

COLONEL *(explodes)* Get out!! I don't ever want to see you
          again!!

> *Ricky eyes the Colonel. He's finally discovered a way to break free from his father, and he can't believe it was this simple.*

RICKY   What a sad old man you are.

COLONEL *(a whisper)* Get out.

> *Ricky grabs his backpack, turns and walks out the door, leaving the Colonel standing there, glassy-eyed and breathing heavily.*

INT. FITTS HOUSE – KITCHEN – MOMENTS LATER

> *Ricky enters to discover Barbara standing in the middle of the room, clutching a dish, frightened. She's obviously heard his argument with his father, and she looks into his eyes, searching, aware that something eventful is taking place.*

RICKY   Mom, I'm leaving.

> *A beat.*

BARBARA Okay, wear a raincoat.

RICKY *(hugs her)* I wish things would have been better for you. Take care of Dad.

> He kisses her cheek softly, then exits out the
> back door, leaving her standing alone, still
> clutching her dish.

INT. FITTS HOUSE – RICKY'S BEDROOM
– CONTINUOUS

> The Colonel's POV: Below us, Ricky dashes
> through the rain to the Burnham's front door and
> knocks. Lester opens it and lets him in.

EXT. FITTS HOUSE – CONTINUOUS

> The Colonel looks coldly down at us from
> Ricky's bedroom window, and then he pulls
> the drapes shut.

EXT. FREEWAY – CONTINUOUS

> The MERCEDES-BENZ ML320 is parked in the
> breakdown lane, its HAZARD LIGHTS BLINKING.
> Cars ZOOM past in the rain.

INT. MERCEDES-BENZ ML320 – CONTINUOUS

> Carolyn sits behind the wheel, listening to a
> MOTIVATIONAL TAPE on the STEREO.

TAPE VOICE —disinvesting problems of their power, and
removing their ability to make us afraid. This is
the secret to 'me-centered' living. Only by taking
full responsibility for your problems – *and* their
solutions – will you ever be able to break free
from the constant cycle of victimhood.

*Carolyn leans over and open the glove
compartment. She takes out her GLOCK 19.*

TAPE VOICE Remember, you are only a victim if you *choose*
to be a victim...

INT. BURNHAM HOUSE – JANE'S ROOM
– CONTINUOUS

*Angela is sprawled across the bed. Jane stands
across the room from her.*

JANE I don't think we could be friends anymore.

ANGELA You are way too uptight about sex.

JANE Just don't fuck my dad, all right? Please?

ANGELA Why not?

*There is a KNOCK on the door.
Jane sits up, alarmed.*

JANE *(angry)* Dad! Leave us alone!

RICKY *(O.C.)* It's me.

> *Jane jumps up and opens the door and*
> *lets him in.*

RICKY *(to Jane)* If I had to leave tonight, would you come
with me?

JANE What?

RICKY If I had to go to New York. To live. Tonight.
Would you come with me?

JANE Yes.

ANGELA You guys can't be serious.
(to Jane)
You're just a kid. And he's like, a mental case.
You'll end up living in a box on the street.

JANE I'm no more a kid than you are!
(to Ricky)
We can use my plastic surgery money.

RICKY We won't have to. I have over forty thousand
dollars. And I know people in the city who can
help us get set up.

ANGELA What, other drug dealers?

128

RICKY   Yes.

ANGELA   Jane, you'd be out of your mind to go with him.

JANE   Why do you even care?

ANGELA   Because you're my friend!

RICKY   She's not your friend. She's somebody you use to feel better about yourself.

ANGELA   Go fuck yourself, psycho!

JANE   You shut up, bitch!

ANGELA   Jane! He is a freak!

JANE   Well, then so am I! And we'll always be freaks and we'll never be like other people. And you'll never be a freak because you're just too perfect.

ANGELA   Oh, yeah? Well, at least I'm not ugly.

RICKY   Yes, you are. And you're boring. And you're totally ordinary. And you know it.

         Angela stares at him, stunned, then starts toward the door.

ANGELA   You two deserve each other.

And she exits, SLAMMING the door behind her.
Jane turns to Ricky and he takes her in his arms.

INT. BURNHAM HOUSE – UPSTAIRS HALLWAY
– CONTINUOUS

Angela sits on the stairs, shaken, crying.

EXT. BURNHAM HOUSE – GARAGE – CONTINUOUS

We're MOVING SLOWLY toward the Burnham's
GARAGE WINDOW through the RAIN. Through
the window, we see Lester, wearing only his
sweatpants, performing bench presses.

INT. BURNHAM HOUSE – GARAGE – CONTINUOUS

Through the window, we see the Colonel standing
outside, watching. We ZOOM slowly in on him as
he watches, transfixed.

EXT. BURNHAM HOUSE – GARAGE – CONTINUOUS

His POV: Lester finishes his last rep, then racks the
weights and sits up, sweaty and out of breath. He
runs his free hand over his chest... and then he
glances at us, suddenly aware he's being watched.

INT. BURNHAM HOUSE – GARAGE – CONTINUOUS

> Lester and the Colonel stare at each other
> through the window.

**EXT. BURNHAM HOUSE – GARAGE
– MOMENTS LATER**

> The RAIN is coming down in sheets now, and
> there is a sharp CLAP of THUNDER. We're
> directly outside the GARAGE DOOR as it slowly
> lifts to reveal Lester smiling at us.

LESTER   Jesus, man. You're soaked.

INT. BURNHAM HOUSE – GARAGE – CONTINUOUS

> Lester pulls the Colonel inside. The Colonel
> moves stiffly and seems preoccupied, slightly
> disoriented.

LESTER   You want me to get Ricky? He's in Jane's room.

> The Colonel just stands there, looking at Lester.

LESTER   You okay?

COLONEL *(his voice thick)* Where's your wife?

LESTER   Uh... I don't know. Probably out fucking that
          dorky prince of real estate asshole. And you
          know what? I don't care.

          The Colonel moves closer towards him.

COLONEL   Your wife is with another man and you don't
          care?

LESTER   Nope, our marriage is just for show. A
          commercial, for how normal we are. When we are
          anything but.

          He grins... and so does the Colonel.

LESTER   You're shaking.

          He places his hand on the Colonel's shoulder.
          The Colonel closes his eyes.

LESTER   We really should get you out of these clothes.

COLONEL   *(a whisper)* Yes...

          He opens his eyes and looks at Lester, his face
          filled with an anguished vulnerability we wouldn't
          have thought possible from him. His eyes are
          brimming with tears. Lester leans in, concerned.

LESTER   It's okay.

COLONEL *(hoarse)* I...

LESTER *(softly)* Just tell me what you need.

> The Colonel reaches up and places his hand on
> Lester's cheek... and then kisses him. Lester is
> momentarily stunned, and then he pushes the
> Colonel away. The Colonel's face crumples in
> shame.

LESTER Whoa, whoa, whoa. I'm sorry. You got the wrong
idea.

> The Colonel stares at the floor, blinking, and then
> he turns and runs out the open garage door into
> the rainy night.

INT. MERCEDES-BENZ ML320 – CONTINUOUS

> Carolyn is still listening to the same
> MOTIVATIONAL TAPE. She holds the GLOCK
> in her hand.

TAPE VOICE 'I refuse to be a victim.' When this becomes
your mantra, constantly running through your
head—
> Carolyn switches the TAPE OFF and puts the
> gun in her purse.

CAROLYN I refuse to be a victim.

EXT. FREEWAY – CONTINUOUS

The Mercedes pulls away from the shoulder.

INT. BURNHAM HOUSE – KITCHEN – CONTINUOUS

Lester enters, opens the refrigerator and grabs a
BEER. Suddenly we HEAR MUSIC coming from
the other room. Lester opens his beer and starts
toward the family room.

INT. BURNHAM HOUSE – FAMILY ROOM
– CONTINUOUS

His POV: As we MOVE SLOWLY around a corner,
Angela comes into view, standing at the STEREO,
holding a CD case. She's been crying; her face is
puffy, and her hair mussed. She regards us
apprehensively... then puts on a slightly defiant
smile.

ANGELA   I hope you don't mind if I play the stereo.

Lester leans against the wall and takes a swig
of his beer.

LESTER   Not at all.
(then)
Bad night?

ANGELA Not really bad, just... strange.

LESTER *(grins)* Believe me. It couldn't possibly be any
stranger than mine.

> *She smiles. They stand there in silence; the
> atmosphere is charged.*

ANGELA Jane and I had a fight.
(after a beat)
It was about you.

> *She's trying to be seductive as she says this, but
> she's pretty bad at it. Lester raises his eyebrows.*

ANGELA She's mad at me because I said I think you're
sexy.

> *Lester grins. He is sexy.*

LESTER *(offering beer)* Do you want a sip?

> *She nods. Lester holds the bottle up to her mouth
> and she drinks clumsily. He gently wipes her chin
> with the back of his hand.*

LESTER So... are you going to tell me? What you want?

ANGELA I don't know.

LESTER You don't know?

His face is very close to hers. She's unnerved—
this is happening too fast...

ANGELA   What do you want?

LESTER   Are you kidding? I want you. I've wanted you
since the first moment I saw you. You are the
most beautiful thing I have ever seen.

Angela takes a deep breath just before Lester
leans in to kiss her cheek, her forehead, her
eyelids, her neck...

ANGELA   You don't think I'm ordinary?

LESTER   You couldn't be ordinary if you tried.

ANGELA   Thank you.
(far away)
I don't think there's anything worse than being
ordinary...

And Lester kisses her on the lips.

INT. MERCEDES-BENZ ML320 – CONTINUOUS

Carolyn drives, her face resolute.

CAROLYN   I refuse to be a victim. I refuse to be a victim.
I refuse to be a victim...

(angry)
Lester, I have something I have to say to you...

INT. BURNHAM HOUSE – FAMILY ROOM
– MOMENTS LATER

Angela lays back on the couch as Lester moves in over her. He pulls her jeans off and gently brushes his fingers over her legs, then moves up and caresses her face...

INT. BURNHAM HOUSE – JANE'S ROOM
– CONTINUOUS

Ricky and Jane, fully clothed, lie curled up on Jane's bed.

JANE   Are you scared?

RICKY   I don't get scared.

JANE   My parents will try to find me.

RICKY   Mine won't.

INT. BURNHAM HOUSE – FAMILY ROOM
– CONTINUOUS

> *Lester starts unbuttoning Angela's blouse.*
> *She seems disconnected from what's happening.*
> *Lester pulls her blouse open, exposing her*
> *breasts. Lester looks down at her, grinning,*
> *unable to believe he's actually about to do what*
> *he's dreamed of so many times, and then...*

ANGELA   This is my first time.

> *Lester LAUGHS.*

LESTER   You're kidding.

ANGELA   *(a whisper)* I'm sorry.

> *A beat. Lester looks down at her, his grin*
> *fading. His POV: Angela lies beneath us,*
> *embarrassed and vulnerable. This is not the*
> *mythically carnal creature of Lester's fantasies;*
> *this is a nervous child.*

ANGELA   I still want to do it... I just thought I should tell
         you... in case you wondered why I wasn't...
         better.

> *Lester's face falls. There's no way he's going to*
> *go through with this now.*

ANGELA *(confused)* What's wrong? I thought you said I was
beautiful.

LESTER *(tenderly)* You *are* beautiful.

> *He grabs a blanket from the back of the couch
> and drapes it around her shoulders, covering
> her nakedness.*

LESTER You are so beautiful... and I would be a very
lucky man...

> *He smiles and shakes his head. Humiliated,
> Angela starts to cry.*

ANGELA I feel so stupid.

LESTER Don't.

> *He hugs her, letting her put her head on his
> shoulder, stroking her hair and rocking her gently.*

ANGELA I'm sorry.

> *Lester takes her by the shoulders and looks at
> her, serious.*

LESTER You have nothing to be sorry about.

> *But she keeps crying. Lester hugs her again.
> We HEAR a loud CLAP of THUNDER outside.*

LESTER *(smiles)* It's okay. Everything's okay.

EXT. ROBIN HOOD TRAIL – MOMENTS LATER

> *The Mercedes pulls onto Robin Hood Trail.*

INT. MERCEDES-BENZ ML320 – CONTINUOUS

> *CLOSE on Carolyn's eyes, reflected in the REAR-VIEW MIRROR. She turns her head to look out the window: Her POV: The RED DOOR of the Burnham house stands out, even in the pouring rain.*

**INT. BURNHAM HOUSE – KITCHEN
– MOMENTS LATER**

> *Angela, once again fully clothed, sits at the kitchen counter. She's eating a turkey sandwich.*

ANGELA   Wow. I was starving.

> *Lester puts a jar of mayonnaise back in the refrigerator.*

LESTER   Do you want me to make you another one?

ANGELA   No, no, no. I'm fine.

He turns to her and cocks an eyebrow.

LESTER *(concerned)* You sure?

ANGELA I mean, I'm still a little weirded out, but...
        (sincerely)
        ...I feel better. Thanks.

A long beat, as Lester studies her, then:

LESTER How's Jane?

ANGELA What do you mean?

LESTER I mean, how's her life? Is she happy? Is she
        miserable? I'd really like to know, and she'd die
        before she'd ever tell me about it.

Angela shifts uncomfortably.

ANGELA She's... she's really happy. She thinks
        she's in love.

Angela rolls her eyes at how silly this notion is.

LESTER *(quietly)* Good for her.

An awkward beat.

ANGELA How are you?

LESTER *(smiles, taken aback)* God, it's been a long time
since anybody asked me that.
(thinks about it)
I'm great.

They just sit there, smiling at each other, then:

ANGELA *(suddenly)* I've gotta go to the bathroom.

She crosses off. Lester watches her go, then
stands there wondering why he should suddenly
feel so content.

LESTER *(laughs)* I'm great.

Something at the edge of the counter catches his
eye, and he reaches for... CLOSE on a framed
PHOTOGRAPH as he picks it up: It's the photo
we saw earlier of him, Carolyn and Jane, taken
several years ago at an amusement park. It's
startling how happy they look. Lester crosses to
the kitchen table, where he sits and studies the
photo. He suddenly seems older, more mature...
and then he smiles: the deep, satisfied smile of a
man who just now understands the punch line of
a joke he heard long ago...

LESTER Man oh man...
(softly)
Man oh man oh man...

*After a beat, the barrel of a GUN rises up behind
his head, aimed at the base of his skull.
ANGLE ON an arrangement of fresh-cut ROSES
in a vase on the opposite counter, deep crimson
against the WHITE TILE WALL. Then a GUNSHOT
suddenly rings out, ECHOING unnaturally.
Instantly, the tile is sprayed with BLOOD, the
same deep crimson as the roses.*

INT. BURNHAM HOUSE – FOYER – MOMENTS LATER

Ricky comes down the stairs, followed by Jane.

INT. BURNHAM HOUSE – KITCHEN
– MOMENTS LATER

*Ricky opens the door from the dining room, then
stops. Jane appears behind him.*

JANE   Oh God.

*Their POV: A pool of blood is forming on the
kitchen table. Ricky comes into the kitchen and
slowly approaches Lester's lifeless body, wide-
eyed but not afraid. Jane follows him, in shock.
Ricky kneels, gazing at Lester's unseen face...
then he smiles, ever so slightly. His POV: Lester
looks back at us; his eyes are lifeless, but he's
smiling the same slight smile.*

RICKY *(an awed whisper)* Wow.

LESTER *(V.O.)* I had always heard your entire life flashes in front of your eyes the second before you die.

EXT. SKY – DAY

> *We're FLYING across a white blanket of clouds.*

LESTER *(V.O.)* First of all, that one second isn't a second at all, it stretches on forever, like an ocean of time...

EXT. WOODS – NIGHT

> *In BLACK & WHITE: Eleven-year-old Lester looks up, pointing excitedly at: His POV: A DOT OF LIGHT falls across an unbelievably starry sky.*

LESTER *(V.O.)* For me, it was lying on my back at Boy Scout camp, watching falling stars...

INT. BURNHAM HOUSE – JANE'S BEDROOM – NIGHT

> *Ricky and Jane lie curled up on Jane's bed, fully clothed. We HEAR a GUNSHOT from downstairs. They look at each other, alarmed.*

EXT. SUBURBAN STREET – DUSK

> *In BLACK & WHITE: Maple trees in autumn.*
> *Ghostly LEAVES FLUTTER slowly toward*
> *pavement.*

LESTER *(V.O.)* And yellow leaves, from the maple trees,
that lined my street...

INT. BURNHAM HOUSE – POWDER ROOM – NIGHT

> *Angela stands in front of the mirror, fixing her*
> *make-up. We HEAR the GUNSHOT again.*
> *Angela turns, frightened.*

INT. SUBURBAN HOUSE – DAY

> *In BLACK & WHITE: CLOSE on an ancient*
> *woman's papery HANDS as they button a*
> *cardigan sweater.*

LESTER *(V.O.)* Or my grandmother's hands, and the way her
skin seemed like paper...

EXT. BURNHAM HOUSE – NIGHT

Carolyn walks slowly toward the RED DOOR, drenched to the bone, clutching her PURSE tightly. We HEAR the GUNSHOT again.

EXT. SUBURB – DAY

In BLACK & WHITE: A 1970 PONTIAC FIREBIRD in the driveway of a suburban home. The SUN'S REFLECTION in the windshield FLASHES BRILLIANTLY.

LESTER *(V.O.)* And the first time I saw my cousin Tony's brand new Firebird...

INT. FITTS HOUSE – THE COLONEL'S STUDY – NIGHT

The Colonel enters, wet. He's wearing LATEX GLOVES. BLOOD covers the front of his T-shirt. He paces in front of one of his GUN CASES; the GLASS DOOR is open, and a gun is conspicuously missing from inside.

INT. BURNHAM HOUSE – HALL – NIGHT

In BLACK & WHITE: Jane opens her bedroom door, staring at us.

LESTER *(V.O.)* And Janie...

EXT. SUBURBAN HOUSE – DUSK

> *In BLACK & WHITE: A door opens to reveal*
> *4-YEAR-OLD JANE, dressed for Halloween in a*
> *Princess costume, holding a lit sparkler aloft*
> *and smiling shyly at us.*

LESTER *(V.O.)* And Janie...

INT. BURNHAM HOUSE – MASTER BEDROOM – NIGHT

> *Carolyn enters, terrified, still clutching her*
> *PURSE. She shuts the door and locks it, then*
> *takes the GLOCK 19 out of her purse. She opens*
> *the closet door and shoves the gun into a*
> *HAMPER. Then, suddenly aware of Lester's*
> *scent, she grabs as many of his clothes as she*
> *can and pulls them to her, burying her face in*
> *them. She sinks to her knees, pulling several*
> *items of clothing down with her, and she begins*
> *to cry.*

EXT. AMUSEMENT PARK – NIGHT

> *In BLACK & WHITE: A younger Carolyn sits*
> *across from us in one of those SPINNING-*

> TEACUP RIDES, LAUGHING uncontrollably as
> she twists the wheel in front of her, making us
> SPIN even faster.

LESTER *(V.O.) (with love)* And... Carolyn.

EXT. PARKING LOT – DAY

> On VIDEO: We're watching the video Ricky
> showed Jane earlier, of the empty white PLASTIC
> BAG being blown about. The wind carries it in a
> circle around us, sometimes whipping it about
> violently, or, without warning, sending it soaring
> skyward, then letting it float gracefully down to
> the ground...

LESTER *(V.O.)* I guess I could be pretty pissed off about
what happened to me... but it's hard to stay mad,
when there's so much beauty in the world.
Sometimes I feel like I'm seeing it all at once, and
it's too much, my heart fills up like a balloon
that's about to burst...

EXT. – ROBIN HOOD TRAIL – DAY

> We're FLYING once again over Robin Hood Trail,
> ASCENDING SLOWLY.

LESTER *(V.O.)* ...and then I remember to relax, and stop

trying to hold on to it, and then it flows through
me like rain and I can't feel anything but gratitude
for every single moment of my stupid little life...
(amused)
You have no idea what I'm talking about, I'm
sure. But don't worry...

FADE TO BLACK.

LESTER *(V.O.)* You will someday.

Afterword
by Alan Ball

I think the idea for *American Beauty* first started rattling around in my head during the whole Amy Fisher/Joey Buttafuoco drama. I was a playwright living in New York, working in the art department of a magazine in midtown Manhattan. On my lunch break one day, I passed a street vendor selling a comic book version of Amy and Joey's story. The cover featured a drawing of a demonic-looking Joey (with a pronounced beer gut) seducing a virginal Amy; on the flip side was an alternate cover with a good Catholic (and much slimmer) Joey spurning the advances of a furious and vindictive Amy as slut from hell. Inside were two equally differing comic-strip accounts of what had happened. This was right after the news had broken of those sad events on Long Island, long before the TV movies started appearing.

I had been just as fascinated, repulsed, and entertained by those events as everyone else, but as I stood there leafing through that comic book, it struck me: we would never know what really happened. The media circus had already begun, and the story was swiftly being reduced to its most lurid elements, with a cast of cardboard stock characters acting on their basest impulses. But underneath it all were real human lives that had gone horribly astray. What had become fodder for jokes on late-night talk shows was to those who had lived it genuine tragedy – and, no doubt, a far more complicated and interesting story than any we would ever hear.

That realization – and an encounter with a plastic bag outside the World Trade Center – was the basis for what would eventually become *American Beauty*. I first started to write it as a play, in which Jane actually did hire Ricky to kill her father because she felt he was just too, well, embarrassing. But it didn't feel right, and after twenty or so pages, I abandoned it. Years later, after moving to Los Angeles and spending four seasons as a sitcom writer, I started working on it again, this time as a screenplay. Before I knew it, it was all I could think about; I couldn't wait to get a chance to work on it. Even if I got home at 3 A.M. (as sitcom writers often do), I'd immediately sit down at the computer and work, sometimes till dawn. It was as if the story had a life of its own, and all I had to do was transcribe it.

I had heard nothing but horror stories of other screenwriters' experiences when their scripts were produced, but I can honestly say that for me the filming of *American Beauty* was a joy. Sam Mendes is not only a brilliant director, he's incredibly generous and collaborative, and coming from the theatre, considers the writer to be an intrinsic part of the process. I was on the set almost every day. One of the most productive times for me (and for the script) was a two-week rehearsal period with the actors prior to filming; they brought depth to the characters I had never imagined, and their insights and suggestions helped immensely.

But eventually, the film began to acquire its own life, just as the screenplay had when I was writing it. Portions of scenes that seemed vitally important on the page suddenly lost their impact, or felt like they were from another movie. Entire sequences were shot, only to be excised later. As Sam observed during editing, 'It's like the movie is letting us know what it wants to be.' The script contained in this book is the script to that film, the film that *American Beauty* became – a better film than the one I originally wrote. What started out as a satire of middle-class American values in the media age eventually revealed itself to be something entirely different, and much more interesting, just like most of the characters in the film. I cannot begin to claim credit for that; it must be shared with Sam, an amazing cast, producers Dan Jinks and Bruce Cohen, DreamWorks, and every single member of the crew.

We live in such a manufactured culture, one that thrives on simplifying and packaging experience quickly so it can be sold. But as Ricky knows – and Lester learns – things are infinitely deeper and richer than they appear on the surface. And although the puritanical would have us believe otherwise, there is room for beauty in every facet of existence.

BIRTHDAY GIRL
Jez Butterworth

John Buckingham was an ordinary bank
employee with a life built on routine
… until he contacted 'From Russia With Love'
and ordered himself a mail-order bride —
who just happens to be gorgeous, speaks
only one word of english 'yes' and
has an insatiable appetite for sex.

Starring Nicole Kidman and Ben Chaplin

• • •

SEXY BEAST

Louis Mellis and David Scinto

Ex-villain Gary Dove has retired to a Spanish villa with the wife he adores. Their perfect lives are shattered by the arrival of Gary's gangster nemesis Don Logan, intent on persuading him to return to London for a big heist.

SEXY BEAST is a genre-bending romance/psychodrama about facing up to the past and the redemptive power of love, and is now a major FilmFour film starring Ray Winstone and Ben Kingsley.

• • •

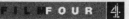